M000044825

LIFTING THE LAYERS TO VIBRANT HEALTH

Detox for Body, Mind, and Spirit

VICTORIA SOL

Important Note to Reader

I am not a medical doctor. The information I offer you in this book is based on years of observation, education and experience only. My purpose is to help you improve your wellbeing. The knowledge I share with you is not intended as a substitute for medical advice or treatment for specific medical conditions. You should seek prompt medical care for any health issues you may have and consult your physician before starting a new diet or fitness regimen.

ISBN: 9780578504643

Copyright © 2021 by Victoria Sol. All rights reserved. Printed in the United States of America. Except as permitted under the United States Copyright Act of 1976, none of this publication may be reproduced or distributed in any form or by any means, or stored in a database or retrieval system, without the prior written permission of the publisher.

Contents

Introduction

Yesterday I was clever, so I wanted to change the world.
Today I am wise, so I am changing myself.
—Rumi

I'm really excited about where you are right now. If you are considering doing a detox, you're probably dissatisfied about something to do with your body and you have a willingness to do something in order to change it. I've been waiting for you. You're the person I am here for and want to connect with. I've been learning, living and sharing this message for decades of my life. It's why I'm here. If I help you make one small change in your lifestyle that improves your health long-term, my work is done. I know beyond a shadow of a doubt that detoxification works, because I've seen it again and again.

The truth is, whether you want to lose weight, heal a health concern, feel more energized, get rid of belly bloat, clear up skin issues, or change your life—celebrate, because change is afoot, my friend. Detoxification is not only effective for changing a current health situation and preventing future illness (which is huge), but the best thing about doing a detox is that it can be the beginning of a life transformation.

I love those words together, "life transformation;" sounds like a magic spell. My first detox changed my life *dramatically*. It was pivotal. I started waking up feeling lighter and clearer. I had more focus. I felt on purpose. I looked more vibrant. It led me to improve my relationships with my family. I changed my career. My life was transformed and it rippled out to everyone around me. Sure, I lost some weight, but the side benefits ended up being so much bigger than I could have imagined. You don't know what you don't know, until you know. You know? Had I known how much I (and everyone around me) had to gain by committing to a detox for a few days, I would have done it sooner.

The fact is, our bodies are rebuilding and regenerating all the time. We have within us the opportunity to realize the health we want, and we can change the course of our lives at any moment. All we have to do is have the desire, the intention, a plan that works, and the willingness to take action and stay the course, even when it's outside our comfort zone.

Since you were called to detox, you obviously have a desire and intention, and you probably also have the willingness to be a *little uncomfortable*. We both know detoxification has a reputation for that.

That's why most people put it off, sometimes indefinitely. This book will provide you with a doable plan that will keep the discomfort to a minimum, but you've got to stick to it in order for it to work.

Repetitive habits are what create our current reality. We don't get fat by eating one unhealthy meal, and we don't suddenly get out of shape by spending one afternoon lazing around. It's what we do or don't do repeatedly that gets us to where we are. I want you to think of a detox like a pattern interrupt, so that the body can heal itself. Another benefit is that you can become empowered to change a few habits that will inevitably transform your life and help you move toward where you want to be—kind of like setting the GPS in your car. You decide you're going somewhere, you set the course, and then you drive until you get there.

Before we can dive into the detox, we first need to explore why we need to detox in the first place. According to *Merriam-Webster Dictionary*, toxins are defined as a small amount of poison, found in air, water, food, and so on. With 20 billion toxic chemicals being released into our environment and food supply every year, there's no doubt that we all need to detoxify.

To detox the body, all you need to do is stop putting toxins in, so that the body has a chance to heal itself. Our bodies, these self-repairing miracles, are always striving toward balance and health—we just need to stop impeding that process and instead assist in it, which is what we will discuss in Chapter 1, A Fresh Start. The next step is to eat a detoxifying diet, which we will discuss in Chapter 2, Detox Your Body. We begin with a detailed plan, which includes what to eat and what not to eat, as well as other helpful seeds of wisdom to make detoxifying more enjoyable and easier.

When I first decided to do a detox, I had 10 extra pounds I periodically lost and regained, depending on how much will power I had to not eat at the time. I had eczema on my face for years that I couldn't get rid of, even after six months of prescription antibiotics that required I stay out of the sun.

The only reason I subjected myself to giving up my favorite foods for green juice and vegetable broth (which was a lot harder than the Lifting the Layers program) was to lose the weight I couldn't seem to keep off and hopefully clear up my skin. I would have been happy with the weight loss alone, but I discovered that I gained a clarity with detoxing like no other. Not only did my skin clear up, but I felt cleaner inside, l had clearer vision, more energy to do things I had procrastinated (like cleaning my closets), and I felt more rested after a night's sleep. I felt like I had lifted a few layers, as though I'd taken off a dirty pair of sunglasses.

The problem was that I gradually went back to my old habits, only to do it all over again when I could conjure the will power. It was like sticking my head in a river of consciousness, but then I'd pull it back out again, knowing that I had enjoyed some cleansing and lost some weight, but it was over now. Time to get back to "regular" life.

After detoxing several times, I realized my mind was calling me back to old habits. I noticed I had "just this once" or "I'll start tomorrow" thoughts. These thoughts are sometimes subtle and more of a feeling than a thought, but always so convincing, because at the time it makes a lot of sense. They worked nearly every time to keep me from making the necessary changes I needed to make, in order to have the physical health and life I truly wanted.

When I took just a few minutes a day to detoxify my mind at the same time I detoxified my body, I felt so much calmer, more centered, and confident after just a few short days. Both body and mind are equally important, because together they have a vibrational impact on our state of being.

Approaching it from that angle, I was simply improving myself on a holistic level and weight loss became a side benefit. I wasn't detoxifying just to lose weight, I was detoxifying to live more fully, to live from the healthy, vibrant person within me that had been covered up for so long. That's why we talk about detoxing our habits in Chapter 3, Detox Your Habits. It sets the stage to show you the value of letting go of your personal thoughts and/or limiting beliefs that have kept you stuck, so that you can practice how to detox the mind in Chapter 4, Detox Your Mind.

At this point, you become more aware of your body from an inside perspective. This is a beautiful thing, because as you begin to feel your inner body, you suddenly realize that you're not as anxious or hurried. You are making more centered and grounded choices. As I practiced this, there was a sense of peace that occupied my body and mind in a whole new way, which miraculously shifted the underlying stress I didn't even know I had until it was gone. It was like I had gotten used to the sound of a loud buzz from a light in my house that I didn't notice anymore until it was turned off. Turning off chronic stress is what we discuss in Chapter 5, Detox Stress.

Life is a continuous unfolding. We are always growing, expanding, and improving. You never arrive and just stay there. It's not as though you get in good shape and never need to work out again. There's always a next level, which is challenging and wonderful all at the same time. It's important to have a stable base as a springboard for life's challenges.

One of the things you'll come to realize as you begin to occupy the body with an awareness of your energetic presence, is that this energy can become obstructed or blocked because of repetition or trauma, both emotionally and physically. These also need to be cleared, which we discuss in Chapter 6, Detox Energy Blockages.

When you know how to clear energetic toxins, you will have taken your health into your own hands in a whole new way.

As we detox, our bodies and minds become clearer, more grounded, energized, and balanced. Then we get the push to clean up our environment, which is really an extension of who we are. Our homes, workspaces, and relationships are always showing us where we need to let some things go—so in Chapter 7, Detox Your Environment, that's what we'll do.

When you've come to a healthy place internally and externally, you realize what an amazing gift everything in life is, and how much you have and want to offer. Life becomes more of a celebration as your life is literally uplifted on a path of transformation. That's what we talk about in Chapter 8, Celebrate Life. A call to detox is a call to transformation.

I've written this book for you. Whether you're trying a detox for the first time or you've done it before, you too can get the most out of detoxification and find lasting change from the effort you're willing to put in. Efficiency, effectiveness, and value are important to me. I want you to get the most out of your efforts. You are the only one who can do this for you. You can't buy a magic pill or pay someone else to do it. You can, however, learn from someone else's experience, and follow a plan that will guarantee results.

So, let's get started.

CHAPTER 1

A Fresh Start

"It has taken time to misguide you so completely,
but it takes no time for you to be who you are."
—*A Course in Miracles*

You are beautiful. Whether you see it or not, you are a beautiful miracle, even if you don't have the physical health or life situation you want right now. Within you, each cell is communicating with other cells with a tiny beam of light that seems to erupt out of nothingness. Many of these cells coalesce into a tangible organ we call the heart, which has an electromagnetic capacity that can be measured several feet away from your body. Your heart pumps 3,600 gallons of nourishing blood through 50,000 miles of blood vessels each day to your other organs. All the while, the heart acts like a sensor that allows you to receive intuitive feelings and experience a range of emotions, every moment of every day for your entire life.

Other cells have merged together to create your eyes, enabling you to see colors, faces, sunsets, and rainbows. When you get a welling up of emotion from the heart, whether pain or joy, tears emerge from these beautiful and miraculous spheres that allow the body to fully feel and express.

Still more cells come together to create the rest of your miraculous body, that allows you to experience love making, music, laughter, and delicious food. All the while, you're actually 99.999% space. If we lost all the dead space inside our atoms, we would each be able to fit into a particle of dust, and the entire human species would fit into the volume of a sugar cube. Yet we run marathons, make babies, surf, paint, go on vacations, and have pets.

While all that is going on, our bodies are continuously being reborn. New cells are born and die in every moment. We have all new skin each month. A broken leg can heal in 6–8 weeks, and a deep cut can heal in half that time. The 3-pound organ we call the liver, that's responsible for more than 500 processes in the body, can repair completely on its own within 30 days, even after 50 percent of all its cells have been damaged.

Because we're always being reborn, and we have free will, we can change. In fact, we are always moving in some direction, toward where we want to go or away from it. Change is constant. You have countless possible future selves, many of which are in a lean healthy body.

The only thing standing between where you are right now and living from knowing that vibrant, beautiful place within you, are the layers of beliefs and habits you've taken on that you confirm and repeat regularly. In some ways, you've been moving away from where you want to go, one moment and decision at a time. Much of it is not your fault. You were just trying to feel good, and in doing so, little by little you moved away from your power source, and adopted beliefs and habits even though they aren't serving you anymore. While you were putting your good health somewhere in the future, you hadn't even realized that you had stopped valuing yourself enough to take care of yourself *now*.

If you came upon a beautiful, luminous flower in the woods, and you could see tiny particles of light continuously flowing out of it, would you knowingly pour acid on it? Would you just ignore it like it was nothing, and keep walking to your next destination? I doubt it. You'd kneel down and marvel at the beauty in it, curious about how it came to be. You'd probably then think about how you could protect it, what you could do to create a safe space for it to grow and flourish. You'd probably take time to tend it carefully and make sure it had enough nutrients, sunlight, and fresh water. I bet you would do whatever you could think of to keep it safe from the environment and other people.

The amazing body that you call your "self," that is reading this book right now, deserves to be cared for as though it were valuable and precious, because it is. You came into this world from a field of pure potential, and you are unique. You were born into this world, but also from it. You came from nothingness. Many cells that emerged from this nothingness joined together, and began the process of creating a body that you present to the world, which is different than the body of any other person in the world who ever was, is, or ever will be.

Human genome testing shows that no two humans are the same. Obviously, they have many similarities, but each human is different from the others. That's hard to comprehend, when you consider that there are 250 births each minute, which is over 4 babies coming into this world each and every second of every minute, of every hour, of every day—each one with a body, mind, and soul. How can there be that much infinite variation continually expanding? The only answer can be that each baby is connected to unbounded pure potential.

Your current reality, in this present moment, is based on every piece of information you have been exposed to and have focused your attention on. After you were born, in an effort to adapt and survive, your body kept recreating itself based on the information it was receiving from everything in your environment, including people, places, and things. Therefore, while you're still part of the unbounded pure potential that you came from, your current body is a tangible result of information you've taken in, from the food you eat, the water you drink, the air you breathe, everything that touches your skin, your relationships, your home and workplace, as well as the thoughts you think, and the emotions you feel about them.

It's time to move toward your wellbeing in all ways: body, mind, and spirit, for we cannot separate the three. Why would we want to? That's like trying to take the magic out of the flower and just look at its petals and stem, totally missing the deeper beauty. Body, mind, and spirit are who we are simultaneously, even when we're sleeping.

This book is *called Lifting the Layers to Vibrant Health*, because that's the way in which getting back to optimum health happens for many of us. Over time, one thing after another falls away, to reveal the perfect being that you are. The beautiful thing is, that all you need to do is stop impeding your body's built-in process of healing, and let nature happen, because you are self-healing.

While my experience of growing up is as unique to me as the 500 pages of genetic code only I possess, you and I have both been in the process of getting to where we are now. We've made decisions and taken action based on what we've seen, heard, felt, and consumed on every level, physically, mentally, and emotionally. Some of these things have limited our experience, and caused us to adopt beliefs and habits. Some of which serve us and others we need to let go of now.

Letting go isn't always easy. It means disrupting the patterns we've become so accustomed to. One of the things that's evident that we need to change is the food we put in our mouths. The reason it's so evident is because of all the current health issues that are clearly related to it, like diabetes, cancer, heart disease, and obesity.

In every moment, you have a choice. You can go on living the way you are, going down the same path, wanting things to be different, but doing the same things you've always been doing. Or, you can in *this moment*, commit to moving toward where you want to be instead.

Sometimes all it takes is a small desire to make a big change. When I was still trying to lose that last 10 pounds after having my second child, I had spent years trying every diet, and looking for the miracle food that would taste good, keep me healthy, and make me slim. I was stuck in the cycle of restricting calories, then overeating because I was so hungry. I'd lost the weight with sheer discipline and gained it back many times. Time and again, I found myself in need of ignoring my body's hunger, so that I could look the way I wanted to look, in order to feel the way I wanted to feel.

One evening after dinner, I was in the kitchen washing the dishes while reading a watercolor postcard I had tucked in the corner of the window over my kitchen sink. I had read this postcard many times, since it was in a place that I often saw it. It was eye-catching, with a beautiful orange and yellow sunrise. It read, "Only as far as I look can I see, only as much as I dream can I be."

I suddenly realized, I had to think bigger. While losing weight was motivating, it wasn't enough. I'd lost the weight before, and while it felt good for a while, nothing had changed. I wanted to feel better. I wanted to have more joy in my life. I wanted to be more confident. I wanted to be a great role model for my children and know how to keep them healthy. I didn't want to continue thinking about my weight anymore. I wanted to live more fully.

Once I birthed that desire, things began to come to me that changed my life. Books like Harvey and Marilyn Diamond's *Fit for Life*, John Robbins' *Diet for a New America*, and Norman Walker's *Raw Vegetable Juices, Colon Health, and Become Younger*. This was the beginning of decades of learning about healing the body naturally and how to eat for optimum health.

I did my first 3-day detox and I was so excited with my results. I continued educating myself, went on retreats, and witnessed detox healing first hand. No wonder Hippocrates, the father of medicine, said, "Let food be thy medicine, and medicine be thy food." This knowledge literally has the power to transform your health.

I was soon witnessing other people's miraculous recoveries. While visiting the Hippocrates Health Institute in West Palm Beach, Florida, I met a man who had gotten the "Go home and sort your affairs" speech from his team of doctors. He and I arrived at the same time and were getting a tour of the grounds together. His skin had a grayish tone, his legs were so swollen that he was in a wheel chair. I stood next to him because he looked like he needed help. At times, he had to get up to maneuver the uneven ground. He was huffing and puffing and resting at every chance. Mind you, this is somewhat standard there. Hopeless medical cases abound.

After three days on the detoxifying plant-based diet, this man was standing erect and walking across campus as though he had drunk from the fountain of youth. The edema in his legs had disappeared and his skin had a vibrant glow. He looked and acted like a new man, like a spell had been lifted. Needless to say, at this point I was a believer. Not only had I seen the physical changes in myself—I was well on my way to my ideal body weight and my skin was glowing—but his recovery was truly miraculous, and it set me on my path.

Suddenly, I wasn't only trying to improve myself; I wanted to share it with the world. I opened my first juice bar, and started teaching anyone interested about plant based living and detoxification.

Your body is always working to detoxify itself. It's like the best personal assistant you could ever ask for. You're walking around throwing stuff at her (or him), "Here take care of this and that, and oh, don't forget that." Your assistant's right there catching things and juggling them, with a running tally of all the things you demand. All the while, your assistant is saying, "Oh, okay. Uh-huh. That too, huh? Okay. Okay. Sure, I'll get to that later. I can put this here for now and that there," while catching the new things you keep throwing.

All you have to do is stop giving your assistant so much to do, so that she (or he) can get to the task at hand. You have to stop the toxins to the best of your ability, so that your body can get caught up. Then, if you happen to throw in one more thing to do in the middle of the day, that's okay. It's manageable. We are bombarded with toxins, physically, environmentally, and emotionally, that affect our health and keep us from living our greatest selves. We need to detox at least a couple of times per year, ideally with the change of each season. More importantly, we need to keep the toxins to a manageable level the majority of the time.

Your liver, kidneys, intestines, lungs, and skin work diligently and continuously to clean up the toxins that you take in from food, water, air, skin care products, and cleaning products.

Your liver is your largest internal detoxifying organ. It weighs roughly three pounds all by itself and it's working on purifying your blood 24/7. It processes, stores, detoxifies, and sends substances back into the blood or to the bowel for elimination. It also stabilizes your blood sugar, metabolizes fat, and keeps your hormones balanced. These are all very important jobs! Your liver alone is reason enough to do a detox, so that it can have a break, and get caught up on its 500 jobs.

When the liver gets bogged down, it often keeps some fat around to safely store toxins until it can get to them later. If measures aren't taken to assist the liver in clearing all those toxins, later never comes.

The kidneys filter about 120 to 150 quarts of blood each day, in order to produce one to two quarts of urine that carries waste out of the body. They make hormones that keep your electrolytes stable and regulate blood pressure.

Drinking water is imperative to healthy kidneys. In fact, if you don't drink enough water, you can end up damaging your kidneys slowly over time or all at once. If your kidneys aren't working properly, it affects your bones, blood pressure, sleep, and energy levels. Make sure you're drinking plenty of water every day.

The lungs are responsible for bringing in oxygen for every cell in the body, also called the breath of life. With the help of the bloodstream, they filter every breath you take, and get rid of toxins in the form of carbonic gas. It's good to be mindful of taking deep breaths in and exhaling fully periodically throughout the day. More importantly, protect your lungs from harmful pollutants (some of which are in your home or office). We'll go more into detail about this in Chapter 7, Detox Your Environment.

Your skin is your largest organ. It's a self-repairing membrane that not only acts as a protective mechanism between your inner body and the outer world, but every tiny cell is constantly sending and receiving information to your brain, based on its interaction with your environment. While it's eliminating toxins, making oil for lubrication and protection, keeping you warm or cool, and allowing you to feel how soft that bunny is, the skin is also protecting you against viruses, and healing itself from trauma and insult at all times.

Last, but certainly not least, the large intestine (or colon) processes waste products and prepares them for elimination. It's important that you have at least one bowel movement each day when detoxing. You don't want old stuff sitting around in your colon on any day, and you'll feel better if you have at least one bowel movement each day. Proper detoxification can be a great way to get you on track.

With more than 80,000 chemicals being used in the United State alone, many of which have never been adequately tested for their effects on human health, there's no doubt we need to detoxify our diet. However, once we get a detoxifying diet in place that allows the body to get rid of stored toxins and begin to heal, the next step is to let go of thoughts and beliefs that no longer serve us, so we can stay the course and eliminate the next layer of toxicity created by self-sabotaging habits.

While almost any detox is better than no detox, detoxing holistically is so much more powerful, because it's more sustainable and has a greater impact. If you commit to detox your body and mind, you will see a difference in your health within the first week. You will begin to see a change in everything else not long after that. Life is a continual unfolding. Even if your health is not a problem, you will always be seeking the next level. While we put so much attention on ourselves, as we get healthier and clearer, we begin to see that the outer body is but a pale reflection (in all its miracle) of what lies inside.

Like waves in the ocean, each and every one of us is part of an energetic whole. What we eat has a major role in that, as does everything we consume regularly. When you stop being a toxin creator and consumer, you not only change your health, you're contributing to changing the world. We live in a supply and demand economy, and we affect each other all the time. When we stop contributing to the problem, there is healing. When we stop consuming toxic products, there's no need for the supply. You have one obligation to yourself, and therefore the world, and that is *to be the best you can be.*

Detox is a call to transformation, because it requires you to step outside your comfort zone, stay the course even when it's challenging, and to be the hero of your own life. In Joseph Campbell's *The Hero's Journey*, the hero gets "the call" (the desire to change). She often ignores it until she feels compelled to act. Then she must step out on her own, not sure of the path ahead. Fortunately, others show up to help (see me waving at you?). She is tested and challenged along the way to her destination, and at some point, she must take a leap of faith. In the end, she is forever transformed and she returns home to share her wisdom with her friends and family.

Most people come to my detox program for weight loss and it will definitely help you lose weight, but if you stay the course with "Lifting the Layers," you not only won't be thinking about how to lose weight again next year during your New Year's resolution, you'll be changing your health forever. Once you stop putting toxins in, (in a short time) your body will heal itself and you will be at a new crossroads. Then, instead of thinking about how you're going to lose weight, you can be deciding what you're going to do with your fit, healthy body—like start a new career, find your soul mate, or move to the home of your dreams.

You are the only one who can do this. No one can do it for you, just like no one can exercise or practice playing piano for you. What you put into it will reflect what you get out of it. Your body, mind, and spirit set the stage for your experience in this life. Being a slave to habits and only staying in your comfort zone is no way to live.

It's time to free yourself.

CHAPTER 2

Detox Your Body

"He who controls others may be powerful,
but he who has mastered himself is mightier still."
—Lao Tzu

So often I get a book, go right to the food guidelines, and skip the rest. I get it. *But* please
know that if you do that with this book, you're missing
the bulk of the information. While following some
guidelines can be helpful in the short term, getting control of your habits in the long run is the real gold. You
wouldn't want to take a penny when you could have the
bank, would you? If you're jumping in right here, go
ahead and put the food guidelines in place, and then get
to the real transformation offered in the rest of this
book. The stuff that will change the game is in how you
think.

The reason I'm so passionate about eating a detox-ifying diet is because I've seen miracles happen because of it. I've watched people lose weight, start a career they love, shrink tumors, look younger, heal MS, fibromyal-gia, and even cancer. Many of them were at the juice bars I owned for over a decade, or the Hippocrates Health Institute in West Palm Beach, Florida. I've been there three times, and I can tell you that most of the people who go there have a serious health concern, and when they adopt the plant-based program, they see re-sults quickly, often within a few days.

If you want to lose weight and gain optimum health, think of food not just for pleasure and to satisfy your hunger, but as information. Our bodies are like chem-istry labs and food is a source of information. Each food will usually help or impede the body's natural healing process. Until you get your taste buds and habits in alignment with good health, think of food as program-ming upgrades for your body and mind.

We often get stuck in ruts based on our taste buds, when they are such a tiny aspect of what food does for the body. Fortunately, taste preference can change by letting go of old habits and adopting new ones, and you don't have to give up pleasurable food. On the contrary, food is meant to be pleasurable. It's just not the only reason to eat it.

We are currently living under a mass hypnosis, as far as diet is concerned. While we know that what we eat is important to our health, we think that the answer to good health is somewhere "out there" when in reality, the answers are only within us. We are all different, and what works for each of us as individuals, only we know best. The problem is, the "out there" answers to our questions are created in order to make someone else money. They're not afraid to do what it takes to make that happen, even if it jeopardizes the consumer's health, like adding extra sweetness in the form of sugar or corn syrup, or extra salt to excite the taste buds and keep the consumer coming back for more. Aside from that, there are additives and preservatives to extend shelf life.

We have inaccurate beliefs around food, thanks to clever marketing. Inaccurate belief number one is that "you gotta get your protein." While eating enough protein is important, most people don't ever have to think about it. It's easy to get enough protein when you eat whole foods. The truth is the body doesn't have to eat muscles to make muscles, any more than it needs to eat eyes to make eyes. We need nine essential amino acids from food; all of which can be found in plants. If you're looking for proof, look no further. I've been living on plants for over 30 years!

What to Eat

Fresh organic raw plant foods need to be the main event when you sit down to eat. They do so much to improve your health in every way, from giving you better eyesight to rejuvenating your liver. Food literally has the power to heal. The fact is, our physiology is made to eat plants. The majority of our teeth are large and flat for grinding things like nuts and seeds. We only have two to four sharp teeth (if that) for ripping and tearing, to bite into apples and other fruits. Our hands are the perfect tools for picking fruit and vegetable gardening.

We have the digestive tract of an herbivore animal like a gorilla. We have roughly 28 feet of intestines, 21 feet of small intestines, and 7 feet of large intestines. Carnivores like lions, on the other hand, have roughly 5 feet of intestines. In fact, all animals that eat other animals regularly (other than humans), have much shorter intestines because meat may contain harmful pathogens, and it will putrefy in the gut if not processed quickly. We lack the proper pH in our stomach acid to digest other animals properly without thorough cooking. An animal who eats other animals has the stomach pH of less than or equal to 1, whereas plant-eating animals have a pH of 4–5, which is what human beings have. Because our pH is higher, foods other than plants can cause more acidity in the body.

Our miraculous bodies neutralize the damaging effect of acidity by holding onto fluid, which is called inflammation. Chronic inflammation is affiliated with arthritis, allergies, skin issues, autoimmune disease, and gut issues. Alkalizing whole foods, like vegetables and herbs, as well as whole food supplements, like blue green algae in chlorella and E3 Live are helpful in offsetting acidity.

It's true; we are designed to adapt. We don't have to always eat *only* optimum foods. We can eat other things and convert them into usable energy, but if we do that regularly, it's at the cost of our health. Instead of nourishing our bodies and providing energy, which is what food is meant for, less than optimal foods can compromise every system in the body, starting with digestion.

The primary reason detoxification works is because, if not impeded, the body heals itself. So, the most important thing to do during a detox is to stop the toxins. The easiest way to do that is to eat an organic plant-based diet. Plants in their natural form are digested in a matter of hours, while animal products can take up to two days, and cause negative side effects like excess mucus and inflammation, which your body needs to deal with, and which takes up precious healing energy. Therefore, by not putting toxins in, you free up your body's energy to eliminate toxins that have been stored there. It's that simple.

Plants are like the symphony for the celebration of life. We so often take their beauty and wonder for granted. It's time to reawaken that sensual experience with your food, because eating is an intimate experience. You take food inside your body, it satisfies and nourishes you, and it's utilized to recreate the body. When detoxifying on a plant-based diet, we diminish acidity, increase alkalinity, give our digestive systems a rest, and up the ante of nutrition.

Not only are plants great for detoxifying the body, but they are also what's best for the environment. They offset emissions and exchange carbon dioxide for oxygen, thereby reducing air pollution, which is also a significant source of toxicity for your body and all other bodies living on this planet. Eating only plant-based foods also reduces the amount of suffering other animals endure, as we get our nutrients straight from the source without taking a life.

Eat Mostly Organic

While consuming fruits and vegetables (even if they're nonorganic) is better than not consuming them at all, it's far better to avoid unnecessary pesticides and other chemicals as much as possible by buying organic. You also want to avoid GMOs as much as possible, and the easiest way to do that is to eat foods labeled USDA Organic, or get your produce from local farmers you know aren't using genetically modified seeds. It's more than likely that if it doesn't have the Organic label it probably contains GMOs.

There is so much debate and confusion about the safety of GMOs, but one truth we do know is this definition in *Merriam-Webster*, "An organism or crop containing genetic material that has been *artificially altered* so as to produce a desired characteristic." When we become aware of this definition, it's easy to understand why genetically modified foods have been called "Franken foods." For an educated consumer, this definition causes discomfort around the idea of consuming it or feeding it to our children, because it's not natural. According to Miles McEvoy, Deputy Administrator of the National Organic Program, in 2013: "The use of genetic engineering, or genetically modified organisms (GMOs), is prohibited in organic products. This means an organic farmer can't plant GMO seeds, an organic cow can't eat GMO alfalfa or corn, and an organic soup producer can't use any GMO ingredients. To meet the USDA organic regulations, farmers and processors must show they aren't using GMOs and that they are protecting their products from contact with prohibited substances, such as GMOs, from farm to table." Whether or not you decide to trust the USDA, as far as how well they actually police this policy, is up to you. My intention is to help you to do your best.

While foods that contain GMOs don't have to be labeled, there is another labeling issue to be in the know about. The word "natural" is misleading, causing many of us (myself included at times) to fall into the trap of thinking something is good for you just because it says "natural." According to the USDA, that word means it doesn't contain artificial ingredients or preservatives, but that doesn't mean it's *without* added chemicals. Therefore, it's best to buy organic whenever possible.

When minimizing toxins, it's best to eat mostly vegetables, some fruits, some nuts, seeds, beans, legumes, and alkalizing grains like quinoa, amaranth, and millet. Also, make sure to include: leafy greens; cruciferous vegetables like broccoli, cauliflower, cabbage, or brussels sprouts; sprouts like broccoli, adzuki, or mung bean; garlic and raw onions; fermented foods like sauerkraut and kimchi; rich colorful fruits like cantaloupe and blueberries; a variety of nuts like almonds, walnuts, or brazil nuts; seeds like flax, hemp, and chia; herbs like parsley, basil, and mint.

Also, include garlic and ginger each day for parasite, virus, and bacteria removal. They are amazing for removing old toxins from the gut and intestinal tract, and for acute illness like cold and flu. You can put them in your main dishes, dips, and dressings. Ginger is great in smoothies, too.

In the beginning, if you're not accustomed to eating a lot of fruits and vegetables, or your digestion is compromised, lean toward more lightly cooked vegetables, then work your way up to including more raw foods. In my experience, eating mostly raw is best for releasing toxins, but eating all raw isn't necessary, and can be difficult to stick to. It can also cause you to feel imbalanced energetically, even if you're careful to use warming foods like herbal teas and cayenne to offset all the cold.

I vary the amount of raw and cooked foods I eat based on the seasons and what's available locally. I utilize more cooked food in the colder seasons and eat more big raw salads during the warmer months. I sometimes have salad for both lunch and dinner with something savory on top, when our farmers market is in full swing.

While detoxifying, eat a variety of plant foods. We can get into a habit of eating the same fruits and vegetables all the time. Often lettuce, tomato, and cucumber make up a typical salad, and while all salad is good, you get more health benefits out of incorporating more variety. Plus, variety is the spice of life; our taste buds need a little excitement, too. Consider eating the colors of the rainbow. Ayurveda and Traditional Chinese Medicine teach us that different nutrients and energies come from different colors, and when we pay attention to eating colors, we pay attention to variety, and are therefore more balanced. Each color contains specific healing properties, like blue foods are great blood purifiers, and orange and yellow foods are great for the immune system. You can use the colors to balance your energy, nourish particular organs, and impact your mood.

Consume 20% sprouted or raw nuts and seeds, as well as raw or cooked alkalizing grains, like quinoa, millet, amaranth, and wild rice). When you eat nuts and seeds, like almonds and flax seeds, you get the omega3 essential fatty acids your body needs. Essential means you need to get it from food; your body cannot make it. These foods are also loaded with a variety of nutrients and all the amino acids your body needs for protein building. I recommend consuming flax or chia seeds every day while detoxifying. When soaked, they have a soothing mucilaginous texture, which is great for keeping you regular. They can soothe constipation and/ or the opposite.

Nuts and seeds are very dense food. You don't need a lot of nuts and seeds, just ¼ to ⅓ cup of nuts, and 1 to 3 tablespoons of seeds per day. All of these foods satiate hunger and provide the body with necessary nutrients for optimum health.

Switch coffee for green tea. I love coffee. It's amazing what coffee can do for you. It can stimulate you to exercise, get more done, start a new project or finish an old one, or be more optimistic in general. The bad news is that coffee is tough on your kidneys, adrenals, and the lining of your intestinal tract, so it's good to take a break from it. Green tea is a great substitute that not only gives you a boost of caffeine, but offers antioxidants that eat up free radicals, and it's alkaline as opposed to acidic, like coffee.

Pay attention to drinking a lot of filtered quality water. Drink at least half your weight in ounces per day. Your body is 60% water and it's always moving. Water is nature's way of flushing out pollution. Think about it like a crystal clean mountain stream, carrying sediment and waste away to be removed. If there isn't enough water or enough flow, things don't stay as clean.

While we're talking about flushing out pollution, make sure you are having at least one bowel movement per day. If you are not, you can add aloe and flax seed to breakfast shakes or salads, or take bentonite clay before bed and again in the morning, according to the directions on the bottle. Water plays a key role in elimination from the colon, as well as from the kidneys.

Consistency Is Key

Like a wave shaping a rock, repetition over time has the greatest impact. A 7-day detox can be a great jumpstart to a life transformation, because it's doable. It's easier to commit to a short period of time, see the impact, and then have a raised awareness about minimizing toxins long term.

A detox can help you get to where you want to be, but your diet is a way of life. It's not something you do for a while, and then return to old habits that got you to where you were before you started. You can use a detox as a springboard, but what you do over time is what makes the difference. As you go through your detox, think about what you can incorporate into your lifestyle that you are willing to continue on a long-term basis. With that said, all you have to do is one day, one moment, at a time.

Look at your food before eating, and imagine where each item comes from, and the process it went through to get to your plate. With each item ask yourself, "Is this food I'm about to bring into my magical being going to bring me more health, or is it going to move me away from it?" Then, pay attention to how you feel in that moment. Your body knows the answer; don't let your mind talk you out of it. If you check in with how you feel when it comes to food, and listen to your body before, during, and after you consume it, you'll be bringing more consciousness into your eating habits, which is where the magic happens.

What to Avoid

Processed foods—any packaged food not in its natural state. Processed foods take a lot of time for your body to digest, and since they usually contain added chemicals for preservation to expand their shelf life, your body has to deal with that, too. It's best to leave these out indefinitely. These include all sodas. Also, trans fat (also known as hydrogenated oils) should be completely eliminated. They are often found in packaged foods for extending shelf life.

Processed meats like hot dogs, ham, sausage, bacon, and lunch meats were named Group 1 carcinogenic in 2015 by the International Agency for Research on Cancer (IARC). IARC is the cancer agency of the World Health Organization.

Sugar should also be avoided as it causes acidity in the body, compromises the immune system, and accelerates the decay process. Need I say more?

Peanuts, corn, wheat, and their products—these foods commonly contain aflatoxin, a fungus which is a toxic compound, which the American Cancer Society recognizes as a mutagenic carcinogen. More and more people are having allergies to these foods, because they are so overused. When you're not detoxing and if you're not allergic, it's okay to eat a little of them, but use them like a treat.

Animal products (meat, dairy, eggs, and fish)— these foods take more time for the body to break down, assimilate, and eliminate the waste. When you consume an animal's muscles, parts, or secretions, you are also consuming what they ate. Just like an infant drinking milk from his mother, you take in every antibiotic, hormone, or chemical the animal had in his or her system when they were milked or at the time of their death. They also cause acidity and tax the body with toxins like bacteria, viruses, parasites, and pus.

When you eat a piece of red meat, your body sends white blood cells to the stomach, as though it were preparing to fight an infection. The IARC also classified red meat (including beef, pork, lamb, and goat) as probable carcinogens.

We are living the consequence of an outdated belief that we need to consume animals for good health, when the opposite is true. We now know that eating animal products is linked to cancer, obesity, and heart disease. In T. Colin Campbell's book, *The China Study*, he describes a study spanning more than 20 years that suggests you can turn up or down the growth rate of cancer cells directly in proportion to your animal product consumption. There have been countless people who have cured themselves of cancer by switching to a plant based diet. When you switch to a plant-based diet, one of the first side effects is weight reduction, which often goes hand and hand with heart disease. That's why Joel Kahn, MD, heart surgeon, and author of *The Plant Based Solution*, jumped on the bandwagon of teaching a plant-based diet for prevention and cure for heart disease, instead of performing heart surgery.

Unfortunately, the meat and dairy industry have a lot to do with the problem. There's money to be made from the mindset that animal products are good for you. When Oprah announced that she would never eat a hamburger again during her show, Texas cattle producers sued her for over $10 million. Their longevity is tied to the US dietary guidelines, thanks to the role they play in the USDA. They continue to promise robust health, even though there's evidence to prove that animal products should be eaten sparingly.

From an environmental standpoint, the effects of animal agriculture are monumental. Industrial animal production is the leading producer of methane emissions. That means that putting meat on the dinner table is worse for the environment than driving a vehicle. Just like our bodies, our world can sustain some toxicity, but it's the overconsumption that's causing the problem. See www.cowspiracy.com for more information.

Even though we now know that eating animals isn't necessarily good for our health, and that it's the biggest contributor of emissions destroying our planet today, the ultimate problem with consuming animal products is that we must turn a blind eye to our compassionate and caring side. Eating a plant-based diet reduces the mistreatment of animals. If you are a conscious consumer, you know all the facts and still choose to eat meat, you can reduce the amount of meat you eat in a day or a week. You can still detoxify a few times a year, as well, and keep the toxins to a minimum the rest of the time.

Most of my family and friends eat meat. That's one of the beautiful things about being a human; we get to choose. The best way to become a conscious consumer is to play detective about the foods you buy, where it's coming from, and how it is tended. Either hunting or buying it from a local farmer who allows you to visit and see how it's being produced is best. Then consume meat modestly. Remember the wave slapping a rock idea; consistent change has the greatest effect.

Once you start eating primarily plants and your body starts cleaning house, toxins begin to be released into the blood stream in order to eventually exit the body, which may cause mild discomfort. The majority of people have nothing more than a slight headache, but there are some who have mild nausea, fatigue, or skin eruptions. Just know that if any of these things happen to you, you're on the right track; better out than in. There's a section on frequently asked questions at the end of this chapter that can help alleviate these mild symptoms without sabotaging your detox. If you experience strong discomfort, you may need to slow the process of detoxification by consuming more cooked whole foods, or having a small amount of coffee, if that's what you're accustomed to.

Exercise

Just like brushing your teeth or taking a shower, exercise should be part of your regular health care regimen. It helps the body get rid of waste by way of the lungs, lymphatic system, and the skin. Deep breathing brings more oxygen into the bloodstream, and therefore all your organs, improving their ability to detoxify and repair. It moves the lymphatic system, a system of fluid that relies on your physical activity to move waste to the kidneys and out of the body. When you exercise, the body perspires, and toxins get pushed out of the skin through the pores, to be washed away in the shower.

When I had all the demands of a single mother of two who owned her own business, I knew how important exercise was for me—not only for staying in shape, but for stress release. The problem was, I felt like I didn't have enough time for both meditation and exercise in the morning, so I bought Shinzen Young's audio CD, "Meditation in the Zone." I would run three to five miles before the kids got up with my headset on and the cassette player in my hand, while listening to reminders to place my attention on different parts of my body, "Feet. . .. Calves. . . Knees. . ." Listening to the CD is helpful, because if your mind wanders, soon you'll be reminded where to place your attention. If you don't have an audio file, you can place your attention anywhere you are currently having a sensation in the body until it subsides. The beauty in this exercise is that it keeps you returning your awareness to your body. The more attention you place on your physical body from within, the more in tune with it you become. The sooner you know when you're going out of balance, the quicker you can remedy the situation.

Even if you hate exercise, there must be something you enjoy that includes movement. The best exercise is the one you'll do. You can count anything as exercise that moves the body: walking, biking, hiking, playing sports, dancing, running, swimming, yoga, golf, etcetera. Rebounding or mini-trampolines are great for moving the lymph, too. In fact, just bouncing up and down gently on the heels helps move the lymph, but a rebounder makes it fun and easy. Try to get one that's sturdy, because if it's not stable enough, it may increase stress and offset the good that bouncing can do.

Lemon Water

Add the juice of one lemon wedge to your water each morning, and then anytime you like throughout the day. Lemon water helps the body detoxify by improving digestion, adding alkalinity, helping you feel more satisfied, and it gives you a small dose of Vitamin C to boost your immune system. Also, the antioxidants help fight free radicals, keeping your skin looking fresh, while helping you produce collagen to smooth out fine lines.

Herbs

Herbs are like nature's medicine cabinet. Not only are they great for giving food flavor, but herbal teas have been considered medicinal for centuries. There are many herbs that assist in the body's detoxification because they support the liver or kidneys, like dandelion or burdock. Others assist in digestion, like spearmint or peppermint, or help purify the blood, like parsley or basil. All of these are beneficial when detoxing. Make sure to add them to your food and drink at least one herbal tea daily.

Fresh Pressed Vegetable Juice

When you're detoxing, or anytime for that matter, you can have fresh juice or replace any meal or snack with juice made from leafy greens, cucumbers, parsley, beets, carrots, celery, or any other vegetables that you like. They are like a shot of nutrition without taxing your digestive system. Imagine how much energy it must take your body to break down the food you put into your mouth, utilize it, and then send the waste package out in the end. Fresh pressed juices are quickly and easily digested, so your body can spend its time getting rid of the old stuff it hasn't had a chance to get to until you started detoxing.

Skin Brushing

Skin brushing is a great way to move the lymph, exfoliate dead skin, and improve circulation, all of which are fabulous for beautiful skin. Skin brush each day before your shower. Gently brush in a circular motion or with long strokes, but always toward the heart, up your arms and across your chest, then up your legs, buttocks, belly, and back. Buy a brush that isn't too coarse; it can be soft and still be effective. Be gentle with yourself. We tend to overdo with the idea that more is better. While hard brushing will exfoliate the skin, it isn't as effective as a gentle touch for stimulating the lymphatic system.

Rest

While some people have more energy during a detox, others need a nap. The key is to listen to your body and rest if needed. Many people enjoy getting to bed a little early after having a light dinner, and wake more refreshed with a flatter belly. If you feel tired during the day, take a quick nap. A 15-minute nap in the afternoon can refresh and restore you better than reaching for caffeine or sugar.

Sauna

Far infrared saunas are amazing for detoxification, relaxation, skin purification, and weight loss. The efficacy of infrared waves is very broad and is a subject of study by NASA. Among the infrared waves, the far infrared rays, which have a wavelength of 6–12 microns, are especially good for the human body. These waves have the potential to penetrate 1.5 to 2 inches or more into the body, allowing for deep heat, which raises your core body temperature from deep inside. Far infrared waves have the longest wavelength, similar to those emitted naturally by the human body. They can penetrate fat cells to vibrate and expel toxins, resulting in the greatest levels of detoxification and potential weight loss. I love my sauna. If you are considering getting one, check out www.sunlighten.com.

Epsom Salt Bath

Taking a bath is not only relaxing for body and mind, but it can help draw toxins from the body. Unlike other naturally occurring salts, Epsom salts are formed from a pure mineral compound containing magnesium and sulfate. Both magnesium and sulfate stimulate detoxification pathways in the body and can be taken in through the skin to reduce anxiety, improve sleep, and promote the health of joints, nerves, and skin.

Bentonite Clay

Bentonite clay is a great way to assist in detoxification of heavy metals, neutralize bacteria, kill viruses, and promote healthy digestion. It has negatively charged molecules that seek out positively charged molecules, which is what most toxins and heavy metals are. The clay binds with them and then removes them from the body. It's great topically, too, in the bath or dabbed onto a skin eruption. When I'm detoxing, I usually take 1 tablespoon in about ⅓ cup water before bed, or you can take 1 tablespoon in water in the morning and evening if you want more. Make sure to drink plenty of water throughout the day when taking this product.

Aloe

Aloe is wonderful for coating the alimentary canal, which is great for a healthy colon and smooth elimination. Elimination is important for everything, but it's a key component for detoxification and radiant skin.

Chlorella

Chlorella has been proven to bind with heavy metals like mercury and cadmium, which can damage the body on a cellular level. Chlorella is also very alkaline, which helps offset some of the acidity in the body created by stress and acidic foods. It also reduces constipation, balances blood sugar levels, and supports the liver, too.

Probiotics

Probiotics are good bacteria that line the digestive tract and support the body's ability to fight infection and absorb nutrients. Most people need to take a probiotic because of poor diet, antibiotics, emotional stress, or consuming GMOs and sugar.

Supplementation

Unless you know you're deficient in something, there's no need to take supplements during a short-term detox, except possibly incorporating aloe, probiotics, blue-green algae, or bentonite clay. Also, there's no need for protein or green powders during a detox. If you eat a variety of plants, you'll be getting the nutrition your body needs.

The only thing I recommend is that if you tend toward low energy and you don't get at least 30 minutes of sunlight directly on your exposed skin every day, you may want to consider a Vitamin D supplement. Most people are deficient in Vitamin D. In fact, the AARP suggests that Vitamin D deficiency is an ignored epidemic and a global health problem

Here are a few recipes to get you started.

Breakfast Shakes

You need a nut or seed-based milk (rice is good, too) or water to make a breakfast shake. I often make my own almond milk. If you prefer, you can use brazil nuts, walnuts, cashews, or other nuts. If you have a nut allergy, you can use seeds like pumpkin, sunflower, or sesame. Creating your own nut milk is fast, easy, and a level-up from store-bought nut milks. Plus, it's inexpensive and fresh. There's no need for added ingredients like sweeteners, binders, or preservatives when you make your own.

If you prefer buying boxed nut or seed milks, make sure they don't have any added sugar.

Nut or Seed Milk

¼ cup nuts or 2 tablespoons seeds of choice (soaked overnight is best, but not necessary)
1 cup of water
1 teaspoon vanilla extract (optional)

Blend on high until frothy.

Once you've blended the milk, add greens like spinach, kale, or romaine, and fresh or frozen fruit. Berries are best as they are loaded with antioxidants and blood purifiers, but you can use any fruits you prefer.

Here are a few of my favorite recipes:

Beautiful Eyes
Orange Walnut Breakfast Shake

¼ cup walnuts blended with 1 cup water
1 whole orange (remove the peel and seeds)
1 cup frozen mango
½ frozen banana

Blend on high until frothy.

Anti-inflammatory
Strawberry Almond Shake

10 raw almonds blended with 1 cup water

1 cup frozen strawberries (8–10)

1 cup baby spinach (you can use more if you like)

1 teaspoon vanilla

4 ice cubes

Blend on high until smooth.

Super Weight Loss
Pineapple Breakfast Shake

2 tablespoons ground flax seed

1 cup water

1/4 pineapple

1 cup frozen strawberries

3 leaves romaine

1/2 cucumber peeled

1/2" peeled ginger root

Blend on high until creamy

Longevity
Brazilian Blueberry Breakfast Shake

46 brazil nuts blended in 1 cup water

1 cup blueberries

1 banana or 1 cup mango

1 cup spinach

3 leaves romaine

Blend on high until smooth

Vibrant Health
Ginger Berry Breakfast Shake

2 tablespoons chia seeds, soaked in 1 cup of water for
15 minutes
1/2'" peeled ginger root
1/2 cup mango
1/2 cup blueberries
1/2 peeled cucumber

Blend on high until frothy

Radiant Skin
Mango Chia Breakfast Shake

1 tablespoon chia seeds soaked in 1 cup room temperature water for 15 minutes
½ cucumber
½ cup frozen mango
½ frozen banana
Blend on high until creamy.

Lunch

A good detoxifying lunch includes a big salad (or
pile of raw vegetables) with something savory on top to
help you feel more satisfied.

Here is a basic recipe example.

Basic Salad

Start with greens and a variety of sprouts, then add the colors of the rainbow.

½ head romaine lettuce chopped (or any other greens you desire)
¼ cup alfalfa sprouts
½ cup pea sprouts
½ cucumber, sliced and quartered
1–2 carrots, sliced or shredded
1/3 cup red cabbage, shredded
½ yellow pepper, chopped
4–6 Kalmata olives (or olives of choice)
½ avocado

Savory Additions:
Quinoa
Steamed vegetables, like broccoli, cauliflower, or green beans
Tempeh
Lentils
Soaked and/or sprouted seeds, like pumpkin or sunflower
Soaked and/or sprouted raw nuts, like almonds or walnuts
Beans, like edamame or navy

Red cabbage salad with walnuts

1 cup red cabbage, shredded

2 carrots, shredded or chopped

1/3 cup walnuts, chopped

1/2 avocado

2 tablespoons creamy garlic dressing

Toss all together and place on a bed of greens

Spinach Salad with Edamame

1 cup cooked edamame

2 cups chopped spinach

½ sliced cucumber

1/3 cup grated carrots

1/2 avocado

Toss together with dressing of choice

Dressings

Dressings are key. Anyone can eat a salad with the right dressing. You want it to be made with primarily whole-foods and taste absolutely delicious. I've often heard people say that they could eat these dressings with a spoon.

Mustard Tahini Dressing

Ingredients:

2/3 cup water

1/2 cup lemon juice

2 tablespoons real maple syrup

1/4 cup stone ground mustard

1/2 cup sesame tahini

2 cloves sliced garlic

1 tablespoon dried parsley (or 2 tablespoons, fresh)

2 tablespoons Braggs Liquid Amino acid

Blend all ingredients in a blender on low until smooth and creamy

Creamy Dill Dressing

Ingredients:

1 cup Vegenaise

1 tablespoon dried dill

2 tablespoons fresh lemon juice

1 pinch salt

1/4 cup water

Put all ingredients in a jar and shake.

Italian Dressing

½ cup olive oil

2 tablespoons apple cider vinegar

2 tablespoons lemon juice

1 teaspoon minced garlic

1 tablespoon minced basil

½ teaspoon granulated onion

1 tablespoon dried Italian seasoning

1 pinch real sea salt

Put all ingredients in a jar and shake.

Creamy Garlic Dressing

½ cup pine nuts

½ cup water

3 tablespoons fresh lemon juice

1 clove garlic

1 tablespoon garlic and herb blend seasoning

2 pinches real sea salt

Blend in a blender until smooth.

Chive Vinaigrette

3 tablespoons lemon juice

½ cup fresh chives, chopped

1 clove garlic, peeled and chopped

2 tablespoons olive oil

1 tablespoon Dijon mustard

½ teaspoon salt

1 teaspoon agave nectar (or maple syrup)

fresh ground pepper to taste

3 tablespoons water (+/− to desired consistency)

Blend in a blender until smooth.

Dinner

During the summer months, it may feel better to have salad twice a day when you're detoxing; but in the cooler months we tend to desire warmer foods in order to stay more balanced and feel more nourished. The idea is to keep it light.

This vegetable broth recipe is one I used in my very first detox. It's ideal for fast weight loss and detoxification.

Vegetable Broth

Ingredients:

1 medium sized head of cabbage

3 large red beets

3 medium sized potatoes

1 large green onion

1 large bunch of fresh parsley

1 small bunch of fresh cilantro

1 bag or bunch of spinach

½ butternut squash (seeds removed)

4 cloves of garlic

3 stalks celery

1 teaspoon thyme

1 teaspoon salt or 1 tablespoon Bragg's Liquid Aminos

Water to cover

Directions:

Roughly chop all ingredients, add to a large pot and cover with water about ½″ above vegetables. If you have other vegetables in your refrigerator that need to be used up, throw them in there, too.

It's good if you have a big enough pot to leave room to stir everything around; if you don't, you can divide it into two pots.

Bring it to a boil, cover, and simmer on low for 25–30 minutes. Turn off the heat and let it sit covered for another 15 minutes. Strain the broth and discard all the vegetable remains.

This usually produces enough broth for several days. If you have broth left over after you're finished with your detox, you can use it in place of water when you cook quinoa or soups.

Watermelon Mint Soup

https://victoriasol.com/watermelonsoup

4 cups seedless watermelon

4–6 mint leaves

4–6 ice cubes

Remove the rind from the watermelon and blend all in blender until smooth. Usually takes about 10–30 seconds depending on your blender.

Creamy Cantaloupe

Ingredients:

1 cantaloupe

1 teaspoon (or more) cinnamon

Directions:

Cut the cantaloupe in half.

Scoop out the seeds and remove the rind.

Place in your blender and blend until frothy.

Enjoy!

Cream of Broccoli Soup

Ingredients:

1 quart fresh water

1 large yellow onion, peeled, halved and sliced

3 Idaho potatoes, peeled and sliced

1 large head of broccoli, remove leaves and bottom half of stalk

1 tablespoon minced garlic

dash cayenne pepper

1 teaspoon salt

2 cups rice or almond milk

Directions:

1. Bring water to a boil

2. Add onion and potatoes and simmer until tender (about 20 minutes)

3. Chop broccoli into bites size pieces and add to stock with garlic.

4. When broccoli is tender remove from heat.

5. Add the rice milk, salt and cayenne.

6. Place half the soup in a blender or food processor and puree. Be careful not to burn yourself.

7. Remove from the blender and pour into a separate pot, puree the remaining half, pour them back to original pot and stir.

When you reheat, reheat over low heat and stir often.

Cream of Carrot Soup

https://victoriasol.com/creamofcarrotsoup

1 ½ quarts fresh water

1 pound carrots, peeled and cut into chunks

1 large sweet potato, peeled and cut into chunks

1 onion, peeled and quartered

¼ teaspoon ground nutmeg (if you have it—if not, okay to omit)

1 teaspoon ground cinnamon dash of cayenne pepper

1 cup unsweetened rice (or almond) milk

2 tablespoons dried dill (or 3 fresh, if you prefer)

½ teaspoon sea salt

1   Bring the water to a boil. Add carrots, sweet potato, onion, nutmeg, cinnamon, and cayenne.

2   Simmer until vegetables are tender (25–30 minutes) Turn off heat and add rice milk.

3   Puree the soup with an immersion hand blender. If you don't have one, you can puree several cups at a time in a blender, taking care to remove the center of the blender top and cover with a folded kitchen towel to protect you from the steam buildup during processing. Place puree in a separate bowl and puree the remaining mix, then return all to the pot.

4   Fold in the fresh dill and salt and adjust seasonings to taste. Serve warm. This soup can be eaten cold, but I personally prefer it hot.

Frequently Asked Questions

Do I have to give up my coffee? Short answer: That would be great. Coffee is a diuretic and it's tough on the adrenals. It's also addictive, so if you can stop, you'll give your body a much needed rest from this stimulant. With that said, you will most likely have a headache if you stop cold turkey. Headaches are thought to be a withdrawal symptom, because caffeine narrows the blood vessels that surround your brain and when you stop drinking it, the blood vessels expand and it puts pressure on your head.

Whatever the reason, it can be uncomfortable. I suggest cutting down on caffeine drastically by switching to green tea. With the small amount of caffeine in green tea, it's likely you won't get a headache and you get all the antioxidant benefits of green tea.

What can I do if I feel a little nauseous? Mild nausea can happen when toxins are being released into your blood stream. There are several things you can try:

- Drink a cup of ginger or mint tea.
- Sniff peppermint essential oil for one minute.
- Try alternate nostril breathing. Pinch your nose closed on the right side with your thumb while you breathe in on the left side, then rest your finger on the left side, while you lift your thumb off and breathe out the right. Repeat, alternating between

    the two for a few minutes. This brings balance to the body and can help with some detox related nausea.
- Eat a quarter to a half an avocado or half an apple, whichever sounds more appealing at the time.

Why do I feel so tired? When your body begins cleaning house, it sends excess toxins into the blood stream to be eliminated. These can include toxins from all sorts of things like chemicals, heavy metals, parasites, and bacteria, which require energy for your body to get rid of. If you feel a little lousy, take it as a good sign and get some rest. After all, resting when you're tired is your body's dream come true. With all that said, mild discomfort is okay, but you shouldn't feel too uncomfortable during a detox. The approach of the Lifting the Layers program is designed to ensure the most benefit without any side effects, but some people have more toxicity that needs to be released, and so it can be mildly uncomfortable.

Should I still take my supplements? If you're taking supplements because you know that you have a deficiency in them, then please continue. If not, it would be best to give your body a break from them while detoxifying.

Can I substitute ingredients in the recipes for things I already have? As long as they are organic fruits, vegetables, nuts, or seeds, you may substitute all you like. For instance, if you have mixed berries instead of just strawberries and you want to use them in your morning shake, then by all means do so. If you want to make a squash soup instead of carrot, as long as your ingredients are whole foods and you don't add dairy or sugar, yes.

I'm hungry after exercising. What should I do?
Go ahead and double up on your breakfast shake if
needed. You can eat as much as you require so as to not
feel hungry for any of the meals. Have carrots and
mashed avocado or celery and almond butter for a
snack. The idea is not to feel starved, but not to get too
full.

**Is this detox just for vegans or people who want
to be vegan?** This detox is for anyone who wants to
transform their health. While weight loss is one side effect, discovering what health means for you and expe-
riencing more peace in your body and mind are the primary purposes of this detox. It's intended to help you
exchange health-depleting habits for more health-af-
firming habits, for long-term transformation. The primary reason to avoid all animal products during a detox program is to minimize all toxins. You wouldn't
want to smear a dirty hand all over your window with
your left hand, while you wash it with your right.

Animals and their products require more energy for
your body to break down and utilize than plant foods,
but perhaps even more importantly, toxins concentrate
in animal flesh. When you eat an animal, you're eating
what they ate, including all the byproducts their bodies
create and store as living consumers of food—and the

emotions created from their life experience, which include: illness, antibiotics, stress hormones, viruses, bacteria, and other microorganisms.

With all that said, living without eating animals doesn't work for everyone, nor does it have to. Once you've given your body a break from them, and you have exercised listening to how your body feels all the time (not just when it's feeling really good or feeling really lousy, try out different eating plans and see what works, while keeping your toxin load down. Try making plants your primary food, because those are the most healing, nutritious, highest fiber, highest water content, health promoting foods.

Isn't it more detoxifying to do a water or juice fast? From my personal experience, as well as my observation of other people doing it that way, it is my opinion that it is far more beneficial to detox regularly over time, by keeping the toxin load down, supporting the body in getting rid of the ones already stored there, and incorporating detoxifying daily habits. That's why I created this program. It's doable and it's not uncomfortable like water or juice fasting. The only real discomfort in detoxifying this way is in letting go of self-soothing habits and taking the time to try new things. These two things are mild compared to not eating solid food for several days. Plus, I know that many people have had great results from hardcore detoxes like that, but they often don't have long-term transformation.

Does everything have to be organic? I can't find all organic in my local grocery store. It's ideal to eat organic or biodynamic, but unfortunately, organic isn't available to everyone yet. If you live in an area where it's difficult to get organic foods, see if you can join a coop, order from your local grocer, or have your organic groceries shipped directly to you. If buying organic is currently out of reach for you as far as cost, you will still gain significant and impactful results from putting the Lifting the Layers plan into practice, even with conventional produce.

What if I'm really hungry while I'm detoxing? You can eat as many fruits and vegetables as you want or need to satisfy your hunger during a detox. A small amount of nuts or seeds usually do the trick if you are still hungry after a piece of fruit. During a detox, the most common time people feel hungry is in the afternoon, and it can be because of a sugar craving.

The important thing is to satisfy your hunger without feeding an addiction or habit. If you feel shortchanged in some way, there won't be a lasting impact. You need to feel completely satisfied while keeping the toxins down and nutrients up. The best way to satisfy a sugar craving is to trick your taste buds. For example, putting cinnamon on apples or eating some sesame tahini works, too. Sesame tahini is loaded with calcium and satisfies a sugar craving for most people.

Yet another reason to do a detox is to free up energy for your body to take care of old stuff. Digestion takes more energy than any other system in the body, so when you eat light, it's logical that your body has more time and energy to work on other things. The key is to strike a balance so that you feel satisfied—not full, but satisfied, or maybe even a little hungry—but not to the point where you're too uncomfortable, because then it's more difficult to stick with it. So, a good way to handle that is to eat a little and give it 10 minutes and then check in with how your body feels. If you're still hungry after 10 minutes, have a healthy snack.

CHAPTER 3

Detox Your Habits

"Everything that's going to come
into creation follows the shattering
of what was there before it."
—*Joseph Campbell*

After assisting customers to detox at my juice bars and doing detoxes myself, the main problem I noticed was that many of us ended up right back where we started, not long after the detox ended. We have a limited amount of self-discipline and we consciously and subconsciously associate people, places, and things with our habits (especially the ones that cause pleasure), until they become ingrained in our everyday life. I know from experience that changing your daily routine, coupled with new habits, works better when you detox the mind and fill up on spirit while living your everyday life. We have habits at home, and in our minds, that need to be undone in order to have lasting change.

Daily habits can make or break your health. You don't get out of shape by skipping a workout occasionally, but you can get into shape by exercising regularly for a month or two. You wouldn't gain five pounds by eating an occasional piece of chocolate cake, but if you ate it every day, you'd have gained several pounds in just a couple weeks. Minimizing toxins regularly has a greater impact than doing an occasional detox, because things add up quickly, just like charges on your credit card. Using a 7-day detox is a great way to set the stage for adopting healthy long-term habits. Once you have a compelling reason to commit to a short-term detox, you've stepped on the path. From there, all you need is to remember your big picture goal to keep you going.

Simon Sinek, author of *Start with Why*, says, "It's not what you do that gets you out of bed every morning, it's why you do it." I couldn't agree more; a good why can get you through. As you embark on this journey, take a broader view. Knowing exactly *what* you want and *why* you want it can help you stay the course when your old habits call you back. Think about it like Harry Potter's "expecto patronum" spell he uses to ward off the dementors (the soul sucking monsters, for those of you who aren't Harry Potter fans).

First, what do you want? Is it to have more energy, heal a health concern, lose a few pounds? That's the beauty of free will, you get to decide exactly what you want, for you.

Second, why do you want it? Is it because you want to have more fun? Is it to feel good in your clothes? Is it to be able to play with your kids? Is it to attract your soulmate? Why do you want it?

Ultimately, everything you do is because you want to feel a certain way, because how you feel is what sets the stage for your experience in life. We're motivated by desire to feel good, whether it's inspired by current pain or a hope or dream for the future. A positive feeling is the real reason to do anything. Ultimately, there's a feeling you want to experience when you've reached the goal of what you want.

How will having what you want make you feel? Will you have more confidence? Will you feel accomplished? Will you be more peaceful? Will you have more love? Will you have more freedom? If the second question of why you want it already led you to a feeling, ask: "How will that feeling make me feel?" to probe a little deeper.

Then come up with your *intention statement* by answering these three questions in this order: What do I want? Why do I want it? How will it make me feel? Put your answers together into one statement. When you've put it together, say it out loud. Notice how it makes you feel, and tweak it until it makes you feel good when you say it. It needs to uplift you a bit, and that is personal for you. If you like the sound of it, but don't notice that you feel a little uplifted from it, spend a little more time arranging the words so that it's believable and a little exciting for you when you say it.

> *Example 1*: My intention for this detox is to lose 10 pounds and change my eating habits, so that I can step into the best version of myself, so that I feel confident and balanced.
>
> *Example 2*: My intention for this detox is to clear up my skin, so that I have more confidence, so that I feel free.

Once you have your intention statement, write it neatly and post it where you'll see it frequently. Read it daily and whenever you feel challenged to stray from your plan. Writing it down not only helps you to remember it, but studies have shown that it's 20 to 42 percent more likely that you'll accomplish it when written. That's right, you can increase your likelihood of success just by writing it down. Now, that's maximum gain for minimum effort. After you've written it, be deliberate about having it with you while you detox and let your body work its magic.

Now, once you've got your intention, think about how long it will take to achieve your goal. Step back and be realistic about how long this will take, then decide on your time frame. Your goal may be to lose five pounds. You can do that in 7 to 10 days while still eating three meals a day, but if you want to lose 20 pounds and get in shape, it will take longer. You decide for you what's realistic and doable. If you don't have any idea how long it will take, start with seven days and assess your progress at the end. Then, set another time frame based on where you are at that point.

Your goal has to be doable or you won't do it. It needs an end date or a day you reassess. When you make your time frame too big, it's easy to put it off because it will always remain out of reach somewhere in the future.

So, you're ready. You've got the motivation, the intention, and the plan. You step on the path and—the world shows up to thwart your success. Your son didn't finish his dinner and you don't want to let good food go to waste. It's just one bite, or maybe two. Your girlfriend asks you out for a drink, she needs you. You want to be a good friend—one drink won't hurt. There are a few cookies left in the snack drawer; might as well just eat them, then you can start fresh. You can always start tomorrow. You deserve a treat; you've been good all day.

I know what it feels like to wake up with the best intentions each morning, only to fall back to old habits by the afternoon. I did this for years, and if that's something you're familiar with, please know that you need to cut yourself some slack and set yourself up for success. You wouldn't leave a pack of cigarettes on your table if you were serious about quitting smoking. We have so many habits built-in to how we live every day. We only have a limited amount of will power and treats are often a form of reward in our culture. So, get rid of temptation in your house. If you don't have the chips in your cupboard, you won't eat them.

Then, take stock of the habits you currently have that move you away from your goal and ask yourself, "Do I really want to stop this habit?" You may think you want to stop drinking coffee, kick the afternoon energy bar or chocolate habit, or stop hitting the snooze button so you have time to exercise in the morning, but what does the habit do for you? Perhaps it brings you comfort or peace or it feels celebratory.

Then, ask yourself, "How is it negatively affecting me?" Perhaps it's keeping you overweight or eroding your confidence because you can't keep your promises to yourself. Maybe it's causing you to feel trapped in a cycle you can't get out of, like a hamster on a wheel.

Then, weigh the two answers. It may be worth it to you to continue having a thick middle if it means you can eat that bag of potato chips that you love each day. When you bring it into the light like that, then you're making a conscious decision. It eliminates the underlying emotion attached to beating yourself up about it, and the inner struggle associated with thinking one way and behaving another. Or, you may feel that the benefit is too small and there is no way you can continue doing it; the cost is too high. Looking at it that way, it's more of a decision than a sacrifice.

If you haven't thought it through and you don't have a definitive decision, you'll easily talk yourself out of it in the moment when the old habit calls. If you decide you want to be rid of the habit, set yourself up for success with a doable plan while you detox it.

Old habits can be undone and replaced with new and pleasurable life-affirming ones. Plan. Plan. Plan. Plan what you'll do when your old habits call and make sure you have everything you need to succeed readily available. Abraham Lincoln said, "Give me six hours to cut down a tree and I'll spend the first four sharpening the axe." When you plan ahead you're more likely to succeed. If you're used to an afternoon snack that you often pick up last minute, like an energy bar, plan an alternative, like sliced apples with cinnamon, and bring them with you. If you usually have coffee with cream in the morning, plan to have green tea with a nut or seed milk instead. Have it ready to go with the green tea on the counter or in your mug, the water in the kettle, and your plant-based milk in the refrigerator.

Have a time line, but remember you only have to choose for right now. This means you are only choosing for *this moment* when it comes to changing your behavior. Use the "now" mindset to choose health affirming action. That's how your old habits have always won—they tell you it's just for right now, it's just this once, or I'll start tomorrow. When you use the "now" mindset to choose health defeating habits, you put your health somewhere in the future. You can't knowingly do things you consider to be damaging to yourself or others today, and expect it to not have an impact on you in the future. The reality is when you do that, you accept the penny because it's right in front of you, while you have the key to the bank in your pocket.

How Do You Detox Your Habits?

When the desire for your habit calls to you, bring your attention inside and look for where you feel it in your body. You may feel it in your stomach or your heart, or perhaps all over. When you find it, focus all your awareness there until the sensation passes. Choose not to act, but just to notice it for this moment. It's not so that you fight against the behavior, but instead raise the awareness within it. Then acknowledge that you brought consciousness into that moment, instead of indulging a habit that you want to break. That's a big success in and of itself.

I became more familiar with the technique of observing physical sensations as they arise and subside during a 10-day silent meditation course called Vipassana. It's the same technique that was taught by the Buddha thousands of years ago, passed down through centuries with the intention of keeping the teaching as pure as he taught it. Vipassana was created to eliminate suffering. In this instance, suffering is created by following your immediate desire, while sacrificing the bigger picture. What I discovered was that when I observed sensations within my body, I could watch them come and go without acting on them. When I did that, there was more space to make a more conscious choice, which meant it was easier to break habits that no longer served me.

Try to observe your physical sensations without judging or labeling. When you judge anything, you are only looking at a portion of the whole. For example, when you look in the mirror and think, "My butt is so fat," you have narrowed your viewpoint to a tiny portion of what and who you really are. It may be true in your current viewpoint that you have a large rear end, but that's just one position based on past programming that created the mindset you currently have.

What if you lived in a culture where big butts were revered and celebrated? Your viewpoint would be different, wouldn't it? I'm not suggesting that you adopt a new viewpoint; just stop and notice how you judge things, and instead just purely observe them like a caring parent watching her child walk for the first time. There's presence and space in the observation.

It may make it easier to stop the habit of judging if you replace judgment with curiosity. When I became curious about my thoughts and feelings, I watched the inner judge who was always finding me lacking in some way. For example, if I said something I wish I hadn't, my inner judge would say something like this in my mind, "Oh my gosh. I should not have said that. I wish I hadn't said that!" There was a feeling within my body of tension, perhaps even a little pain in my chest, my throat would clench, and I even stopped breathing for a few moments. Then I remembered to be curious about it, and that would go something like this, "Breathe. Wow, that's interesting. Why would I say that? I wonder what's behind that. Hmm . . ." The response to that more curious thought is that my body was more relaxed, and it helped me stop berating myself or seeing myself as flawed.

When you get curious about your sensations, thoughts, and feelings, you may notice there's a deeper underlying feeling there, such as unworthiness. In fact, unfelt emotions like unworthiness can keep you stuck in a pattern of self-loathing and self-soothing, which shows up as health depleting habits. Unprocessed emotions can subconsciously drive you to do things you don't want to do. We'll talk about clearing unprocessed emotions in Chapter 6, Detox Energy Blockages.

When you become aware as an observer of what you're thinking and doing habitually, things begin to change. In the ancient wisdom texts, known as the Upanishads, this is called "being the lamp at the door." I love this analogy, because the lamp illuminates the way to see more clearly. That's it. There's no need to figure out the lamp's past or make a story about the lamp. It just is. Either it's illuminated or it's not.

Occasionally ask yourself:

- What am I thinking?
- How am I feeling?

Mind and body are intertwined. We'll discuss this more in the next chapter, but from a physiological standpoint, and as far as habits go, the body has sensory neurons in every organ. When it's accustomed to a certain diet, it will send messages to the brain to get more of what it's used to, even if it isn't good for you.

When you start detoxing your habits, there may be times you forget and find you're peering in your snack drawer or even eating the snack. Whenever you do remember, you have brought more consciousness into your life. Once you are aware of it, you can see it for what it is. "That's my body calling out for what it's used to," and, "As I become conscious, I have a choice."

Just like when you have drunk too much alcohol and you have a hangover the next day, or as a heroin addict experiences withdrawals when they stop using the drug, as toxins begin to leave your body you may experience a headache, body aches, fever, or other flu-like symptoms. You may also experience emotional mood swings and food cravings, because your body has gotten used to certain foods and is in the habit of receiving them.

When you bring in more awareness and detox the habits you no longer want, you can move toward where you want to be with more ease. When you don't act on these urges for a while, and at the same time replace old habits with new ones, your body will get used to it, and then the desire diminishes.

When subjects at Monell Chemical Senses Center in Philadelphia were shown the names of foods they liked, the parts of the brain that got excited were the same parts activated when an addict had taken their drug of choice. Perhaps more importantly, neuroscientist Dr. David Shelton and his team at the University of Rochester found nerves throughout the body initiating messages to the brain. The job of a nerve fiber is to transport impulse sensation to the spinal column. They act as both information receivers and senders to get the body to take action.

Soon you can begin to look at your own behavior from a bigger perspective in an inquisitive way. What does this person "I" call "me" do every day, from morning to night? Am I making choices that will lead me toward where I want to go or *away* from it? Am I spending my time doing things I actually enjoy? If I knew that I would die tomorrow, would I be spending my life this way? What would I do differently?

We live as though we already know everything about ourselves, but there are countless things we don't know about the body and some incomprehensible things we do know. For example, if the DNA in your body were uncoiled it would cover 10 billion miles, that's about from Earth to Pluto and back again.

The study of human anatomy can be traced back thousands of years, yet it's still uncertain why we have fingerprints or an appendix. The truth is, you don't have to know everything about how the body works. A more important focus is what the mind is doing. When you catch the thought or feeling that pulls you toward your unwanted habit, stop and recognize that you caught yourself, and give yourself some love. You deserve it.

CHAPTER 4

Detox Your Mind

"The mind is everything.
What you think you become."
—Buddha

I f you've lost the weight you wanted to lose before, but slipped back to old habits and gained it
back again, or if you feel stuck and can't seem to lose
the weight no matter what you eat, detoxifying your
mind can change the game for you.

According to the research of Dr. Fred Luskin of
Stanford University, "A human being has approxi-
mately 60,000 thoughts per day, 80% of these are negative and 90% of them are thoughts you had yesterday
and the day before." I'm sure you've heard this estimate
too, and like me, couldn't actually wrap your head
around it (no pun intended). It's such a big number that

it doesn't seem realistic, but even if it were a tenth that many, wouldn't it make sense to detox a few of the most harmful repetitive ones?

Of course, the real reason to detox a thought is because it has a negative impact on your life experience. It would be great if we only had thoughts we chose, but the mind introduces all kinds of thoughts that we don't necessarily want to think. You know this to be true when you wake up in the middle of night and you can't get back to sleep, because you're worrying about your child, your work, or your health. Or when you're involved in an activity like doing the dishes and a thought comes in that makes you feel sad, because you're remembering a disturbing story you heard in the news.

The first thing I noticed when I began to watch my thoughts was that it was true, I had a lot of them. I was a freshman in college, embarking on my first meditation course. The professor instructed us to watch our breath as we sat on an industrial tiled floor, facing a blank white wall with the lights turned off and no windows in the room. My mind wandered continuously, and with good reason. First, I was terribly uncomfortable. I had broken my back when I was 14, so sitting on a cold hard floor wasn't doing my body any favors. Second, the big round clock positioned above the door to the room kept calling me. The window at the top third of the door allowed just enough light in to make out the location of the big hand, as I peeked every few minutes in disbelief about how little time had passed between thinking about *watching my breath*, my grades, my bills, my job, *watching my breath*, my friends, my homework, my family, and *watching my breath*. Even though it seemed like maximum effort for minimum gain, I did come to realize that these were just thoughts passing across my screen of awareness. More importantly, I didn't have to get caught up in everything I thought. I could at times, choose to just watch my thoughts and even choose to let them go.

Our thoughts are often like a continuous river that pulls us along with no regard as to whether it's helping or hurting. It just is. Often whatever is going on in our mind, has completely taken over our attention, and we forget what it is we want to be thinking. We're just thinking and feeling whatever is coming to mind. Why this is important is because, thoughts and feelings create not only our emotional state, but also our physical reality—more than enough reason to detox repetitive damaging thoughts.

> "How we see the world determines our biology."
> —Bruce Lipton, cell biologist and
> author of The Biology of Belief

There's a new science on the scene called epigenetics. Actually, it's not that new (it's about 100 years old), but it's currently getting a real foothold in our collective way of thinking. *Epi* means "above," so epigenetics means "above genetics;" in a nutshell, there is something above your genes that controls whether or not they express. Biologists have come to know that genetics are not the deciding factor of our physical bodies, even though the current limiting mindset that perpetuates our victim viewpoint is that genes are the deciding factor of our physical bodies.

When scientists began to look at why some people carrying the same gene expressed a particular trait and others did not, they discovered that it's the environment the cells are in that decides what the cell becomes. This explains why you may carry a particular gene, but do not have the physical expression of it and your sister does.

Bruce Lipton saw this first hand in his petri dish experiment, where cells of bone, skin, or organ became whatever the fluid in the dish was. He also concluded that both lifestyle and thought patterns are significant in creating cell environment within the body and that, in fact, *lifestyle and thoughts* decide the fate of the cell's genetic expression. We know that lifestyle is key for health: eat your vegetables, exercise, rest, think happy thoughts, and so on. The deeper understanding here is: a thought is translated by the nervous system into a chemical response in the body. Said another way, how we see the world creates chemicals in our body, which bathe our cells, and cause our bodies to express wellness and illness.

Denis Waitley, motivational speaker and athletic trainer, is famous for saying, "If you go there in the mind, you'll go there in the body." You may have seen him in *The Secret*, where he talks about attaching electrical sensors to athletes to measure the physiological response to running a race only in the mind, while sitting in a chair with their eyes closed. They discovered that the same muscles fired as if they were actually running the race even though they were sitting still.

If you have thoughts that are causing you to hold on to your weight, like, "I'm so fat. I'm destined to be overweight because my mother is overweight," "Ever since I went through menopause I can't lose weight," or, "I have to give up all the foods I love in order to be thin," you're creating your reality.

You're actually bathing your cells in that directive to continue to hold onto or even gain weight. Even if you don't have the conscious thought anymore, if you believe that and it's a feeling you have, you're still directing your cells to hang onto the weight.

Thoughts and feelings are intertwined. Our thoughts create how we feel, but also how we feel creates our thoughts. The best way to know what thoughts you need to detox is to recognize the most repetitive ones that cause the worst feelings.

It wasn't until many years after I first began watching my thoughts that I realized that my thoughts were the deciding factor for how I felt, and I could decide if a thought served me, or if it needed to be detoxed. I practiced disassociating from repetitive toxic thoughts that caused negative emotions—or kept me stuck reliving the things I wanted to change, like losing weight, getting healthier, improving my relationships, or doing work I love.

The first thought that I detoxed was that I wasn't a good enough parent, because it was the one I knew caused me the most frequent pain. When I was pregnant with my first son, I set out to be a great Mom. I read parenting books, took college courses in early childhood education, and paid careful attention to what other mothers were doing, in order to be deliberate about what kind of mother I wanted to be. But like most mothers, I did things I regret. When my oldest son went to college, sometimes regret filled thoughts would just come in, while I was doing a mindless chore like folding laundry. Thoughts like, "I should have been home with them when they got home from school, instead of having a babysitter every day while I worked" or "I should have taught them to cook dinner with me and made it fun." These kinds of thoughts were magnetic to other regrets, and guilt was like a muddy rut in the road that sucked my vehicle in every time. It didn't have to be a conscious thought; it was a bad feeling of not doing it good enough and I was living a life sentence. That is, until I detoxed it.

The difference between positive thinking and detoxing a thought is that you're intentional about letting the thought go that no longer serves you, before shifting to the one you want to think instead. You bring your awareness to what's happening in the present moment, feel it fully, intentionally let it go, and choose the new thought. Positive thinking can be merely shifting from a negative thought to a positive one, which can be helpful, but the lasting change that can happen when you actually *detox* the habitual thought you no longer want to think, before planting the new one, is like weeding the garden.

Here's why this detox idea works. When you catch a thought, and disassociate from it by recognizing it's just a thought instead of believing it, it begins to lose its power over you - the power you gave it.

We have a choice. We don't have to let the mind think us. Neuroscience tells us that when you take in new information, a new pathway is created in the brain. If the new information causes a powerful emotional reaction, it happens even faster, and it can impact how you perceive things in the future. If you practice catching non-serving thoughts and replace them with ones that serve you, you can strengthen new pathways to create new habits. The unused pathways dwindle until they are like an overgrown footpath in the woods. You will never completely forget them, but they won't be like the highway to your experience.

It's time to stop putting your good health in the future. If you were heading in the wrong direction on your way to your destination, you'd redirect and change course, simple as that. You wouldn't be hung up on the turning around part, procrastinating turning around day after day. Once you figured out a way to begin heading in the right direction, you'd just do it. You might be upset for a while that you spent so much time heading in the wrong direction, but after you turned around you'd focus on the road ahead and your issue would be behind you.

That's what a detox can do for you. It's a pattern interrupt that helps you to head in the right direction. The only effort that's required is to direct your attention. This is why getting your mind on board, as part of the redirect, is so important. Otherwise, you may find yourself headed in the wrong direction again.

Your self-fulfilling prophecy is playing in your mind. In the last chapter, we talked about the fact that you are living the physical reality of yesterday's thoughts, beliefs, and behaviors. What you think and do today defines your tomorrow. The thoughts that you think lead to the choices that you make, which lead to your experiences. The beautiful thing is, you have control of your mind. You just need to practice it like playing an instrument or learning a new language. Make today the day you stop old limiting thoughts and turn the situation around. Once you break free from the boundary of where you are now, you have a new starting point.

> "Our life is the creation of our mind."
> —The Dhammapada

In 1992, *the Southern Medical Journal* described a case of a man diagnosed with liver cancer and given just months to live. After his death, an autopsy showed that his tumor had not grown or spread one bit since his diagnosis. His doctor wrote, "Could it be that, instead of the cancer, it was his expectation of death that killed him?"

Every action that got you to where you are was first a thought or a feeling. This is neither good nor bad in and of itself. When it's a problem is when it's making you unhappy, or keeping you from living fully, by putting the life you want somewhere in the future. Things like, "It's just this once," or "I'll start tomorrow," are thoughts that waste your time, and can wreak havoc on your health and wellbeing.

The primary thing obscuring your highest self is the negative thoughts and beliefs you repetitively think and feel. It's time to detox them so that you can be more of who you're meant to be. Then, you can deliberately choose what you want to think instead.

It is through training the mind and choosing consciously that we can change our lives. The mind is the middle ground between unbounded pure potential and the manifest world. Therefore, it's the most powerful tool we have available to us, because it taps us into our essential nature, which has unbounded potential, and bridges the gap from the nonmaterial to the material world.

In order to be deliberate, you need to know what you want. If you can't state what you want, you can discover it by defining what you don't want—clarity through contrast. You experience health concerns, jobs and relationships that show you what you don't want, and they cause you to know more fully what you do. For example, your first relationship may have failed because you were attracted to that person based on how they looked, but after you've been with them for a while, you realized that this person doesn't share your love of adventure or appreciate being in nature as much as you do. Before too long, you realize that what you really want is someone who shares your values and interests.

Once you know what you want, be deliberate about heading toward it as often as possible. Keep stepping back into the observer before you make a decision. When you are purely observing, you can make a choice from a still place that is already pure abundant health.

You can choose from the deepest, most conscious part of you that will be with you no matter what body you're in, whether it's young, old, heavy, slim, healthy, or ill. You, as the observer, have control to decide which thoughts serve you and which thoughts you will detox.

The mind is always introducing thoughts about the past or the future, and when you're watching it, deciding what you want to keep and what to toss, you get to choose.

Shift from following your inner saboteur to being your higher self. Not all self-sabotaging thoughts need to be detoxed; some just need the babysitter. For example, I don't particularly care to exercise, but I know I feel better afterwards and it's good for me, so I do it. Even though I'm committed to exercising four or five days a week, at times my mind will still try to talk me out of it with things like, "I'm too tired or I'll do that later" and later never comes. The truth is, I know I need to exercise and my inner saboteur just wants to be comfortable, so I say to myself, "I know, but just for right now we're going to exercise," as I put on my sneakers.

One thing you may notice as you change your diet, is the sense of limitation that comes in to thwart your success. If you happen to go out to a restaurant while you're detoxing (which I strongly suggest you *don't* for at least the first week), plan ahead and repeat your intention for your end result before entering the restaurant. Fortunately, there are many more healthy options than there used to be, but it will be easier for you if you plan ahead and look at the menu online to discover what they offer that fits into your plan.

Again, the mind creates your experience. Shift to noticing that you get to eat delicious food prepared by someone else. See yourself walking out of the restaurant feeling better than when you walked in. If instead you're unprepared, you might walk out feeling like you ate too much and thinking you need to change your life tomorrow, maybe start exercising or stop drinking. Remember, this is your choice and you get to choose. For right now, you're choosing to detox and step into a healthier, more vibrant version of yourself. It's not forever, it's just for right now; it's just for this moment. This is expansion. Limitation is having the desire to experience something different, but never doing anything about it.

The ability to observe your thoughts is the first step to discovering the thoughts you want to detox. If you're always caught in them and they decide your reality, you're not using the greatest tool you have available to you, your awareness. Being able to pay attention to what you think and detoxing unwanted thoughts is the ultimate door toward more freedom, joy, and peace.

Meditation

The energy that creates everything is flowing through us, and we are born with the power to direct it with our minds. The first step is to get quiet within. That's where meditation comes in. Meditation is the ultimate tool for training your mind. Think about it like taking your multivitamin. It covers the bases. It's an anchor for your practice in life. Meditation is the practice of placing your attention on the part of you that's aware you're having thoughts. There are many ways to meditate.

A Few Meditation Technique

> Ask yourself repeatedly, "Who am I?" Often, when you first begin, you'll have all sorts of answers and none of them can capture or define you. They are about you. The real you is behind all that. The process of asking, "Who am I?" can take you there.

> Or . . .
> Sit comfortably with your spine erect and focus on your breath, your inner body, or a mantra (a word or sound, like Om), then bring your attention back to what you're focusing on whenever you realize your mind has wandered. This is the practice of meditation. Many people think they're not doing it right, because their mind keeps wandering and

can't get quiet, but you can't do it wrong. It is a practice of redirecting your attention whenever you notice your attention is lost in thought. Gradually over time, your spaces between thoughts expand and the mind becomes quieter.

Or . . .

Guided meditations can help you begin to practice focusing your attention. They are a great way to bring your awareness inside to the nonphysical part of you with a guide reminding you to pay attention.

How to Catch Self-defeating Thoughts

Generally, a thought that needs to be detoxed is either one that makes you feel bad in some way or is going to take you away from where you want to go (your intention statement). You may notice it causes a physical reaction in your body, like sweaty palms, racing heart, heart pain, or a sudden jolt of energy. Others are just quietly self-defeating. They cause you to feel low or erode your self-confidence.

You may discover when you begin detoxing thoughts, that some have become limiting beliefs. A belief is just a thought that you've come to believe, perhaps because you've thought it many times. It may or may not be true. It's just something that you live by, like I'm not good enough or I can't do that. When you begin to practice self-inquiry, and unravel limiting beliefs, you begin to detox the mother lode of toxins you've been carrying around in your mind, often without even realizing it.

Just like there are ways to assist the body in detoxing with diet, reducing stress, and cleaning up your environment, there are ways to detox the mind of toxic repetitive thoughts and unresolved emotions, like: hypnotherapy, Emotional Freedom Technique, and Neurolinguistics Programming. I've come up with a simple way that works right in the moment, too.

A Step-by-Step Thought Detox Process

- Bring your awareness to the thought you have chosen to detox.
- Notice if you feel it in your body. If not, just hold it In your mind.
- Imagine shining a bright light on it until it is cleared.
- Replace it with the new thought you would like to think instead. Start with something simple that's believable for you.
- To solidify the new thought in your awareness. Think it whenever you remember to while your

awake and doing other things, but especially first thing when you wake up in the morning and right before you go to bed at night.

- Whenever you catch yourself thinking the old thought that you're detoxifying, think, "There it is." Then follow these steps, shine the light on it until it disappears and replace it with the new thought.

Example of a thought you want to detox: "It's just for right now," or, "I'll start tomorrow." Catch it, then go through the steps above and whenever you notice you have the old thought again, remind yourself of your new replacement thought.

Example of a replacement thought: "I'm making healthy choices now. I'm well on my way to abundant health."

Tips:

- Every so often, bring your attention inside your body. We'll talk more about this in the next chapter.
- There is nothing that tastes as good as being healthy and slim feels, but you don't have to be perfect. When your detox is over, you will occasionally have something that is not detoxifying and that's perfectly okay.

- Keep your written intention statement with you. The world is demanding your attention all the time. When, you keep the end result in mind, choices seem easier.

- Shift from surviving to thriving. In challenging situations, ask yourself, "What do I really want?" "What would be the ideal way for this situation to work out?"

- Remember to repeat your new thought or affirmation throughout the day to strengthen the new neural pathway.

CHAPTER 5

Detox Stress

"The field is the sole governing
agency of the particle."
—Albert Einstein

Experts are saying that we endure stress an average of six hours a day, and depending on what you do, it could be more. Chronic stress can impact your life in countless ways. It interferes with sleep, sex, digestion, and of course the body's ability to handle toxins. In fact, stress is the number one cause of digestive disorders, and if your body isn't digesting your food properly, it either stores it for later or gets rid of it without utilizing all its nutrients. And as an added bonus, you age more quickly when frequently stressed, because your physiology is damaged during the stress response.

For years, I lived in a chronic state of stress. The only problem was, I didn't know it. It had become my status quo. There were times I recognized that I needed to slow down, but then I'd get right back to the task at hand.

I was a single parent, running a new business. Fortunately, my saving grace was that I had my diet figured out and I enjoyed what I was doing, but owning a juice bar before it became cool was a demanding lifestyle. To make ends meet, I managed every aspect of the business and worked behind the counter most days from open to close. I'd get out of bed early enough to exercise before the kids got up, get them ready, drop them off at school, go to work for the day, come home in the evening to relieve the babysitter and make dinner for the kids, get them to bed, then do the administrative stuff for the business, like payroll, menu planning, and marketing. I rarely took a day of and if I did, there were things I had to catch up on, like bookkeeping.

But isn't that how it goes? You fill up your life and then you have a full life. Having a lot (or even too much) to do isn't the real problem. The real problem is the sense of urgency that causes you to feel hurried, always behind and like you're lacking in some way, because you could always do it better if only you had more time. Never mind taking time to relax, unless you've collapsed in front of the television for some mindless entertainment—maybe even munching on mood soothing snacks because they calm your stress hormones. Perhaps you're finally on that one week vacation you take each year, but you're sick.

The thing is, your body will eventually say, "Hey, enough is enough. I need a break." And you get the flu or tweak your back, and you end up at the doctor's office or on the couch, which is not only costly and inconvenient, it's painful.

An estimated 75–90 percent of all physician office visits are for stress related issues. We live in a fast paced and stressful world. We often feel like we do too much, but then in other ways, we feel like we don't do enough. We should exercise more, spend more time with our children, eat healthier, or start that project we just don't have enough time. Most people feel like they do too much and don't do enough simultaneously.

As we covered in the last chapter, the brain is constantly adapting and rewiring itself. The bad news about that is that chronic stress can change your brain, rendering it less coherent, diminishing clarity and mental performance. The "stress hormone," cortisol, is believed to create a domino effect that hardwires pathways between the hippocampus and the amygdala in a way that can shape neural pathways in the brain to become predisposed to a constant state of fight or flight. In that state, you're not thinking clearly; instead, you're in a reactionary state. The good news is that you can heal this situation and rewire the brain by creating new pathways, new ways of thinking that reduce the number of stress hits you get each day.

While stress can be offset with exercise, time off, body work, massages, or naps (and all are good), a daily practice to quiet chronic stress can be more effective, because even on vacation or while getting a massage, you can have an issue going on in your life that you can't seem to get off our mind.

The first step to detox stress is, again, to stop the toxins. Just like with diet, be deliberate about what you consume in the form of information. The media, TV, movies, magazines, books, and conversations can all trigger stress and have a lasting impact by storing toxins in your mind and therefore your body.

Thich Nhat Hanh teaches, "When we watch television and movies, we consume; when we listen to music or a conversation, we consume. And what we consume every day may be highly toxic."

Sometimes the things we choose for entertainment can be causing a stress response in the body. I remember watching horror movies as a teenager. It was fun to crouch down low in the theater seat, pressed against my friend, as the victim on screen got into bed oblivious to the person hiding beneath them, or managed to get into the shower not noticing the intruder behind the door. But like a night of drinking too much, each time afterward I felt physically hungover, and would have to go for a walk or listen to music to offset the downward feeling from all that adrenaline coursing through my veins.

We get hits of stress all day long from things we choose to pay attention to, and things we just happen to be in the vicinity of at the time. Our news is primarily focused on the negative, with our government in such disarray, terrorism, cancer rising, global warming, natural disasters, education costs, as well as the social challenges our children face these days. We are consuming a lot of information that can be toxic and cause serious stress.

We have the fight-or-flight response for good reason, but we're still in the process of not letting it overtake our current reality. If you were on your morning run and you suddenly came upon a vicious dog that had gotten loose and began chasing you, this response would be very helpful. What happens when the body is in a stress response is that the blood rushes to the limbs to give you a heightened capability to fight or run. Your platelets become more sticky, in case you get cut and start to bleed. Your heart rate speeds up. Stress hormones increase and the immune system becomes weakened, because at that point, the body's primary concern is to save itself from the immediate threat. Healing, repair, and detox functions take a back seat.

Fortunately, we don't usually have to worry about being attacked, but we do have the same stress response when engaged in upsetting conversations with other people, or when someone dangerously cuts you off in traffic, or even when someone's unkind to you or your family. Anytime you feel threatened in some way, your stress hormones increase. A buildup of stress inhibits the free flow of energy and information; the more stress you accumulate, the less efficient your mind and body become.

When they finally realize it's a problem, most people turn to meditation to reduce stress and anxiety, to quiet their minds, and develop a calmer approach to life, because it works. It has been proven that physiologically, meditation has a dramatic effect on stress. In one study, a group of 46 veterans suffering from PTSD were taught to meditate. They were divided into two groups, one that meditated twice per day and the other meditated once per day. Both groups showed significant results after practicing for only one month. All participants showed drastic decreases in PTSD symptoms, but the group that meditated twice a day had even better results.

Many people think they can't meditate because they think they need to stop thinking, but meditation is not about stopping your thoughts. You cannot stop thinking. It's about resting in the stillness behind the thoughts. Thoughts will always come and go. They will, at times, take your attention and that's okay. It's part of the process. In fact, it's a beneficial part of the process, as it strengthens your ability to redirect your attention, and it's a form of stress release. The more you can learn to observe your thoughts and watch them go, the less stress you keep in your body.

Meditation calms the sympathetic nervous system, which calms the fight-or-flight response and turns on the parasympathetic nervous system. During meditation, the body shifts to a state of restful awareness in which we see the opposite effects of stress; the heart rate decreases, blood pressure normalizes, breathing becomes more quiet, stress hormones are reduced, and the immune system becomes strengthened. In the long run, the deep rest we experience during meditation helps the body support greater balance and vitality.

After practicing meditation for a while, the mind becomes more quiet, even when you're not meditating. One advantage to that is that you don't take threats as seriously, unless they are truly dangerous. You can take the time to respond to a situation and think more clearly. I have heard many people say this has happened to them after meditating even for a short time, plus they slept better, because their mind was quieter.

Meditating will result in many good things; you'll notice you feel calmer or you're not as quick to become irritated during the day. The calmness that comes with meditating gives you the opportunity to make a deliberate choice in the moment, which can lead to a more joyful life.

While it helps to practice meditation for even a few minutes each day, bringing presence to your breath and inner body throughout the day can give you beneficial moments of calm and relaxation.

It's proven that we can deliberately use the mind to turn the stress response off, and bring peace and harmony back inside the body. A group of collaborative doctors and scientists at Harvard Medical School devised a system to "feedback" information about blood pressure levels to a group of monkeys. These monkeys quickly learned how to deliberately lower their blood pressure in order to get a reward or avoid a punishment. In another one of their studies, non-meditators were able to lower their blood pressure at will by thinking relaxing thoughts.

Herbert Benson, Founder of the Mind/Body Medical Institute at Massachusetts General Hospital and founding trustee of the American Institute of Stress, coined the term "relaxation response." The relaxation response is not a technique, but a name for the physiological responses that happen when the parasympathetic nervous system (also known as the rest and digest system) is activated, which is what happens during meditation. This " relaxation response" is used at the Beth Israel Hospital in Boston as a therapeutic way to counter stress.

Coining it the "relaxation response" is a great way to utilize meditation, even if you think you can't meditate.

Here is a meditation process, which elicits the body's "Relaxation Response":

- Sit quietly in a comfortable position.
- Close your eyes.
- Deeply relax all your muscles from your feet to your face.
- Become aware of your breathing and while breathing easily, repeat the word "One" on the out breath.
- Continue for 10 to 20 minutes. You may open your eyes to check the time, or set a gentle bell as a timer.
- When you finish, sit quietly for a few minutes, at first with your eyes closed and then later with your eyes open before getting up.

Another valuable resource comes from the Heart Math Institute, which has been researching stress reduction through the heart–brain connection for years. They came up with this "quick coherence technique," which they have proven to help reduce stress right in the moment. They define coherence as "an optimal physiological state shown to prevent and reduce stress, increase resilience, and promote emotional wellbeing. Coherence is measured through heart rate variability

(HRV)—a unique window into the quality of communication between the heart and brain which directly impacts how we feel and perform."

- Focus on your breathing.
- Drop your awareness into your heart.
- Elicit a positive feeling that you have felt before.

In my experience, when I bring my awareness inside my body and pay attention to my breath throughout the day, it not only decreases stress, but I have created space to change my behavior and respond to situations from a more deliberate position.

Practicing body presence naturally helps you feel more calm, centered and grounded. The wonderful thing is it takes no time at all, because you can do it anytime, anywhere, even while you're doing something else, like listening to someone speak, standing in line at the grocery store, or watching a movie.

Whenever you "go unconscious" and move away from what you really want in the big picture, that's when you need presence to bring you back to the choice you're making in the moment. As often as you can, check in with yourself and return your awareness to your inner body, particularly when you're in a challenging situation. When you do that, you can begin to unravel automatic responses to reach for things that comfort you habitually. These comforts may include: eating junk food, watching too much television, drinking too much alcohol, or anything not in alignment with your dream of how you want to be.

> ## Cultivating Awareness of Your Inner Body
>
> Here is a guided practice to feel the presence within your body. You can listen to the guided audio here: www.victoriasol.com/bookaudio. Once you've practiced this a couple of times, you can bring presence into your body on demand while you're doing other things.
>
> Please sit comfortably with your spine erect and your hands resting in your lap. After you've practiced this once with your eyes open to read, try it with your eyes closed.
> Now raise your right hand in front of you, elbow bent about heart height, palm facing in and relaxed. Keeping your eyes closed, put all your attention on that hand and feel the energy within it. Breathe and keep your attention on your hand. Can you feel it? It may feel a little tingly.
> Now raise your left hand to face the right, with some space between like you're holding a softball. Feel both hands at the same time. Now bring your awareness up your arms into your chest and shoulders, then up your neck into

your face and head. Hold your awareness there for a moment. Breathe into it, and be sure your shoulders, neck, and face are relaxed. Feel the energy in your face, all the way up to the top of your head.

Return your hands to your lap and bring your awareness to your feet. Now bring your attention up your calves and shins, into the knees, both back and front of your knees. Move your awareness up into the thighs, and up into your pelvic area. Feel the tip of your spine and abdomen.

Now we're going to create a loop up the back and around to the front. Feel your buttocks. Bring your awareness into the lower back, then up the spine to the back of the shoulders and neck. Then move your attention up the back of your head and around to the top of your head. Now feel your face. Move your awareness down your neck, into your chest and down into your belly. Now, feel your entire body, from the top of your head to the tips of your fingers and toes.

Hold that awareness in your entire body. Take a deep breath and exhale. Again, take two more deep breaths and exhale them out.

Whenever you're ready, gently open your eyes. Rest aminute or two before getting up.

If you didn't feel the energy in your hand during the meditation, close your eyes and ask yourself, "Can I feel my hands?" If you continue intending to feel your hands, eventually you'll notice that you do. It can be very subtle, so you may think you're missing something. If you can feel where your hands are without looking at them, you'll notice there's a presence there. Sometimes it takes a little time and practice, and that's okay. In fact, when you do feel it (and if you practice, you will), you'll have something to celebrate.

CHAPTER 6

Detox Energy Blockages

"Nothing ever goes away until
it teaches you what you need to know."
—*Pema Chödrön*

A whole-body detox would not be complete without talking about the energy body. Everything is made of energy: the food you eat, the clothes you wear, the house you live in, the chair you're sitting on. There is nowhere that energy is not. It is in you and around you. In fact, it is you. These waves of energy vibrate at a certain frequency and have an impact on each other all the time. It's part of your experience, whether you realize it or not.

Perhaps we should have started the book here, because energy is the basis of everything, and just like the stream of thoughts that come into your awareness, even though you can't see them, you have the power to manipulate them. Realizing this power within us is so fundamental to living a full life that it should be taught to our children from the beginning of their education, along with how to take care of the body, be in relationship, and stay present.

I tell you this from an eternal skeptic's position. We're hardwired to be skeptical of the things we cannot see or the things that seem "magical." The idea of the nonphysical energy body seems easy to discredit, because it's subtle and we're primarily focused on the physical world. I was so skeptical that I still had a hard time believing in the power of energy healing, even after performing it with my own hands, and seeing the results with my own eyes. I struggled with belief even after I used it to heal a herniated disk, after being told by two specialists that the only way out of pain was surgery.

When I had a herniated disc, each night I would wake from the pain after lying down in bed for a couple of hours, and I'd have to get up. I had so much sciatic pain from my back, down my buttocks and into my leg, that I couldn't step on the floor or put my pants or shoes on. My husband had to help me get dressed. I couldn't get comfortable walking, lying down, or sitting.

One thing is for certain, pain is motivating. I went to doctors, chiropractors, physical therapists, and an acupuncturist (and I hate needles). I took anti-inflammatories and wore magnets. I'd do or try anything anyone suggested, because I was consumed by the pain and the desire to heal it *as soon as possible*.

Finally, I began to think, "I'm fighting it too much; just relax," and that seemed to help, but only a little. I began imagining energy running up my spine and clearing out the injury, and then sending healing energy into it.

One day as I finished my meditation, I heard the word "Cheegong". I didn't know what it meant, nor could I remember hearing it before. I asked my massage therapist about it, and then later in the day, my acupuncturist. They both told me it was a form of exercise and I should give it a try. After exploring Qigong, I realized that I had been practicing it intuitively already by running the energy up my spine. All that was needed was a more focused effort and in a few weeks, I had healed my herniated disc.

Believe it or not, even that experience didn't have me fully believing in the power of energy. The most miraculous and compelling healing I experienced was when I used it to heal chronic lymphedema in my right arm. I had had it for so long, the skin had begun to deteriorate on my forearm and hand. My wrist and elbow were in pain and I was limited in what I could do with it. I hadn't seen the bones in my wrist or the veins in my hand (as were so prominent on the left arm) for years.

I couldn't wear short sleeved shirts. I was embarrassed, discouraged, and in disbelief that this could be happening to me.

After spending years and thousands of dollars trying to find a solution, I flew across the country to the only lymphedema specialist at the time. I needed to know why this was happening to me; I was very healthy otherwise. The best guess she had as to the cause was that I'd overused my forearm, elbow, and wrist through repetition working in the juice bar all those years. She had the technology to run a test and see what was going on inside, and I jumped at the chance.

I waited in the waiting room for the radioactive material that would be used for the test. When the delivery person arrived with a square metal box with a big skull and cross bones on the side, I was in disbelief. Was I really going to do this?

With hope of finding a solution, I watched the radioactive material be injected into the puffy skin on top of my hand. Then I exercised to move the lymph and we waited for the material to move up my arm so it could be detected on the imaging machine to see what was going on in my lymphatic system. When we viewed the images, it showed the material had stopped at my elbow, which caused the doctor to conclude that the lymph nodes in my armpit were dead.

That's when I was told for the third and final time; there was no cure. The only possibility was to do what some women who've had lymph damage after breast cancer do, and have surgery to replace the lymph nodes in my armpit. The lymph nodes would be taken from somewhere else in my body and relocated under my arm. She wasn't a surgeon, and said the surgery may or may not be successful. She felt that since I had such a great diet and I was extremely healthy otherwise, I could continue managing it with compression sleeves and elevation, never lifting anything over five pounds. She said that I should wear a bracelet with a warning that I had this condition, so that if I ever became unconscious and needed emergency care, they would be careful not to puncture the skin, because I was at high risk of infection for the rest of my life.

I had learned to live with it for over five years, until one day when I was exercising, I looked at it and thought, "Why not try Qigong on it?" I began sending the energy through it and seeing my arm back to its slender size, bones, veins, and all. I looked at my left arm for reference, then I focused on my right arm, while sending the energy from my shoulder out my hand like a garden hose. I continued to clear it and imagine it healed each day for about two weeks, until one day I realized the swelling was completely gone. Soon after, the skin returned to the same health as my left arm, and it has stayed that way ever since. I often forget that I ever had the problem in the first place.

Qigong

Qigong is an ancient practice of cultivating energy. It's based on the idea that we have energy flowing through our bodies, supplying every cell like an electrical supply to a factory. If the factory receives the electricity, it functions properly and can make the products it's supposed to make. The goal of an individual studying Qigong is to learn to sense the energy, develop it, and control it. Like learning to play chess, only a few minutes are required to learn the basic principles, then you can play chess for pure fun or you can spend a lifetime mastering it. As the student learns more, further subtleties can be perceived, allowing understanding to deepen and broaden.

When something interferes with an energy flow it's called a blockage. These blockages can be caused from repetition, trauma, or emotional stress. Whether the cause was internal or external, the result is the tissues of the body now have an area that may have poor energetic circulation. In either case, Qigong is a method for removing these blockages and improving the energy circulation of the body.

You can think of it like a rock that rolls into a stream. When a rock rolls into the stream, the water begins to be diverted around it. The rock is then causing some areas to not get enough water and others to get more than they should. Qigong is a tried and true method to remove the rock and retrain the energy to flow along its original proper path.

In China, medical Qigong students must pass a test after years of practice, to show that they can change the pH level in water, and leave a hand impression on a piece of paper without touching it, just by holding their hand over it. You don't have to do any of that. In fact, you don't even have to believe it works. Just stop believing that it doesn't. You probably don't know how your eyes produce colors, yet you see them. All you have to do is try it wherever you have pain or blockage in the body. You can do this on someone else's pain or problem, and even your dog or plants can benefit.

We talked about where your attention goes, energy flows. That is the basis of Qigong. The steps are simple and like playing an instrument, the more you practice, the more you can feel the energy. Please visit www.victoriasol.com/bookvideo to see the video of the method below.

A Basic Qigong Exercise
to Clear Energy Blockages

We are going to start with shaking. If you can do this from a standing position, great. Stand with your feet hip width apart. If you need to be in a seated position, that's fine, too. Either way, relax and begin with one leg and just shake it out. Imagine all the negative emotions, trauma, or pain just exiting out through the bottom of the foot. Shake one leg, then the other leg, then shake your arms, torso, neck, and head. Continue relaxing and gently shaking for a minute or two. Imagine all the stagnant energy releasing though the bottom of your feet into the earth.

Now, if you have any area that experiences pain or discomfort, maybe your shoulder, lower back, or your knee, you can focus on that area. If you don't have any particular place in your body that needs attention, you can send the energy to your kidneys for longevity, your abdomen for strong digestion, or your face for a youthful glow.

You can begin clearing the area. In Qigong it's called "combing," because you use your fingers like a comb. Imagine you have long fingers extended about a foot beyond the tips. Use these long fingers to comb through the area you want to clear (or detox). Always comb in a downward stroke and out the hands or feet on the same side of the body. This combing is clearing the blockage energetically.

Do this a few times until it feels like you've completed that area. You'll just get a sense that you're done, like a gas pump when it turns off. You might feel a small click or release. There is no specific time requirement. Trust what you feel. Once you've cleared, get ready to send energy there.

Now, clap your hands together and rub them briskly, until you feel some heat and energy, and place your hands on the place where you've decided to send healing energy. Imagine the energy flowing from the environment or the sun into the area through the top of your hands. Feel it flowing through your hands, but keep your attention on the area you're clearing or healing. If you have more than one place on your body that needs extra attention, clap your hands together again, rub them briskly, and send energy into the next area. You can do this for as long as you'd like, but do it each day for at least a minute or two. The more you practice, the better you'll get at keeping your energy clear and healthy.

When you're done sending to each individual location, take your hands and scoop the energy up and around over your head. As you bring your hands down slowly, feel the energy in your body from the top of your head, down your neck and shoulders, down your torso and your hips and buttocks area, then down your thighs and knees, and out your feet. Scoop up again and repeat one more time. When you're finished, bring your feet together. Take a deep breath as you scoop your

hands up over your head and place your palms together in a prayer position. Exhale as you bring
them down in front of your heart and bow to yourself.

Clearing by Intention

Because the mind leads the Qi, a definitive decision can
begin to clear an old pattern of emotion, trauma, or
blockage as well. Dr. Bernie Siegel, a former medical
professor at Yale University, discovered that merely deciding to let go of grudges and past grievances with
other people can have a dramatic impact on your body
all by itself.

He stated, "I have collected 57 extremely well doc-
umented so-called cancer miracles. At a certain particular moment in time, they decided that the anger and
the depression were probably not the best way to go,
since they had such little time left. And so, they went
from that to being loving, caring, no longer angry, no
longer depressed, and able to talk to the people they
loved. These 57 people had the same pattern. They gave
up— totally—their anger, and they gave up—totally—
their depression, by specifically a decision to do so. And
at that point the tumors started to shrink." For more
information about his work, go to www.berniesiegelmd.com.

Emotional Energy Blockages

We have been programmed to seek pleasure and avoid pain for our very survival. Doctors Rick Hanson and Richard Mendius say in *Buddha's Brain*: "In order to pass on their genes, our animal ancestors had to choose correctly many times a day whether to approach something or avoid it. Today, humans approach and avoid mental states as well as physical objects; for example, we pursue self-worth and push away shame." It's natural to move toward what pleases us and away from what doesn't. The problem is when there is an emotion that comes up and we try not to feel it. These emotions can become "trapped" in the body, because emotions are energy too.

Have you ever gotten sick after eating something, and then for weeks or months you couldn't imagine eating that thing again? In fact, when you thought about it, it made your stomach cringe. This is an example of memory stored in the body.

How to Clear Emotional Energy
Before It Becomes a Blockage

When you get an emotional hit, perhaps something has just happened and you feel anger, sadness, disappointment, or resentment. Usually you'll feel it in your stomach area or your heart, but some people feel it in their throat or shoulder. The first step is to bring your awareness into the body and feel it. Relax the body and feel the emotion more fully, then imagine moving it through you and out your feet or hands. You can physically move your body. You can cry, or if appropriate, yell—whatever you feel inspired to do in order to intentionally move it.

Then notice how you're feeling again. After you've processed the emotion, bring in the opposite feeling—the feeling you would prefer to have.

For example: If you're feeling angry, after you've processed it, you might choose to bring in understanding. Have patience with yourself and give yourself some time to shift. I've heard that it takes 90 seconds to fully feel and process an emotion, but I would say it depends on how strong it is for you. If you can look at it as an observer, that alone can help you feel a bit better, then you can process it instead of storing it.

If this process doesn't give you enough relief, you may want to try Emotional Freedom Technique, which is tapping the meridians while thinking about the issue. There are many teachers of EFT, but a thorough understanding with examples is available in the documentary called *The Tapping Solution*.

CHAPTER 7

Detox Your Environment

"You attract and manifest whatever corresponds to
your inner state. Your inner world
and outer world are one."
—*Eckhart Tolle*

O ne of the side benefits of detoxing the body is that as you get clearer, there is a natural urge to detox your environment. You may get the urge to clean out your closets and drawers, get rid of those piles in your office, or even change a relationship you've been dissatisfied with for years. This is a huge topic and I could write an entire book on this part alone, but for the sake of this book we're going to go broad.

Environmental toxins include all toxins outside your body, which means anything that touches your skin or comes in contact with your energy field. In fact, it's impossible to avoid all environmental toxins, but you can limit them so that your body has a better chance of handling the ones you can't avoid.

This chapter will give you an array of ways to limit immediate environmental toxins.

Once you become aware that there are 20 billion toxins in the environment, it can be discouraging and seem hopeless. Don't worry, your body can handle some toxins, it's just the overload that can cause a problem. Taking a few steps in the right direction can make a big difference to your toxin load, and that's really all you have to do. Just take the first step and keep stepping toward where you want to go. It's the little things that add up over time that make all the difference in regards to where you end up.

Start by getting rid of the products you use most often that contain potentially harmful chemicals. Look at your cleaning products, skin care products, soaps, deodorants, lotions, makeup, and feminine products. Studies suggest that the average woman has exposed herself to up to 515 chemicals during her morning bathroom routine. Your skin absorbs what you put on it, and those chemicals get inside your body and need to be dealt with. When you put something on your skin, think of it like food for your body. You wouldn't eat a plate of food if you had no idea what it was, or if you knew it contained poisonous ingredients. Reading ingredients is important to begin to raise awareness around what you consume. Just know that the companies that create beauty products, including skin care and cosmetics, are virtually self-regulated. It's totally legal to create products with cancer-causing ingredients, and companies do it all the time. They don't even have to disclose all their ingredients. Often, if an ingredient gets the media's attention as being carcinogenic, you'll suddenly see packaging that says it's free of that toxin, like "PABA Free" or "BPA Free." Once the awareness dies down, the harmful ingredient remains in many products that say nothing about it.

A good rule of thumb is to keep it simple. Look for products that don't have a lot of ingredients, especially ones you can't pronounce. As you buy new products to replace the old, look for ones that have a short list of ingredients, or ones that are locally made or at least organic (or biodynamic), and cruelty free. You can get them from a local herbalist or farmer's market, at your local grocer or health food store, or make your own.

Widely Used Carcinogenic or Harmful Ingredients

- **Parabens** are used to prevent bacterial growth in cosmetic products. The side effect is that they are known to mimic estrogen and cause breast cancer.
- **Synthetic colors** in cosmetics are carcinogenic and are linked to ADHD in children.

- **"Fragrances"** is a term used to keep a company's formula a secret. Fragrance mixes have been shown to cause allergies, dermatitis, respiratory distress, and possible effects on the reproductive system.

- **Phthalates** are chemicals found in a number of skin care products. They are known endocrine disruptors, and are linked to breast cancer, as well as reproductive birth defects in both males and females.

- **Triclosan** is another known endocrine disruptor, linked specifically to thyroid and reproductive hormones. It can be found in toothpaste, antibacterial soaps, and deodorants.

- **Sodium lauryl sulfate** is an ingredient to make things foam, like toothpaste and shampoo. It's found in more than 90% of personal care and cleaning products. It has the potential to interact with other chemicals forming nitrosamines, which are carcinogenic. They can also lead to kidney and respiratory damage.

- **Formaldehyde** is used in cosmetic products to prevent bacterial growth. Formaldehyde was deemed a human carcinogen by the International Agency for Research on Carcinogens (IARC), but it's still widely used in household cleaning products and cosmetics by other names with the roots "formic," "methyl," and "methylene." Formic aldehyde, methyl aldehyde, and methylene glycol are a few examples.

- **Propylene glycol** is a petroleum based ingredient that's considered safe, so it's widely used in moisturizers, sunscreen, makeup products, conditioners, shampoo, and hair sprays. It seems only a matter of time before it becomes a recognized carcinogen, as it's already recognized as a skin irritant, and it causes problems in the cardiovascular, neurological, and respiratory systems.

- **Sunscreen chemicals such as benzophenone, PABA, avobenzone, homosalate, and methoxycinnamate** are easily absorbed endocrine disruptors and are also linked to cancer. Healthy sunscreen alternatives typically include ingredients like zinc oxide or titanium dioxide as a physical barrier to protect the skin from the sun.

Cleaning Products

Start with your laundry soap, because you're wearing this cleaning product on your clothing all day long and then in your sheets all night. Next, replace your multipurpose cleaner, dish soap, and floor cleaner. Switch to organic, nontoxic, environmentally friendly cleaning products. My favorites are orange, coconut, or enzyme based. A few powerful ingredients to use in cleaning products if you want to make them yourself are: tea tree oil, vinegar, orange peel, and lemon oil. They work well and they smell fresh and clean.

Unfortunately, it's less expensive for manufacturers to make harmful products rather than healthy ones, so the natural ones can be pricier in comparison. An inexpensive and easy to make all-purpose cleaner recipe for your home includes: equal parts water and white distilled vinegar, plus 20 drops of essential oil like lemongrass, peppermint, or orange. I use this on my counters, stove, refrigerator, floors, everywhere. It saves me money, works like a charm, and smells clean. Make it in a small bottle and use it up. It tends to lose the fresh smell if it sits around too long.

Don't be fooled by clever packaging designed to charge more money by making you think it's a healthy choice. Just like with food, the phrase, "All natural," is sometimes used on skin care and cleaning product packaging. The word natural does not take into account the production methods, such as the use of pesticides, or if the product contains harmful ingredients, or if they have any health benefits. Some companies use the word "green" or create a natural looking label to compete with truly healthy products www.ewg.org/skindeep is a website you can use to look up products to see if they're toxic.

Air Quality

First, stop the toxins. Make sure there isn't mold growing in your walls or carpet, if you live in a humid area. A new carpet can actually be more toxic than an old one, because of all the chemicals that outgas from some new carpets for years to come. Hardwood floors are a better option, in terms of air quality. If you need to clean an old carpet, get it professionally cleaned with a nontoxic cleaner, as conventional cleaners may contain toxic chemicals. Then, get yourself an air purifier for your bedroom. Hopefully you spend a good chunk of time sleeping, and when you are sleeping you take deep relaxed breaths. Making sure that your air quality is exceptional for at least this much of your day can have a drastic impact on your health. Aside from that, the soft white noise produced from a good air purifier can help you to sleep more soundly for a longer period.

Water

www.ewg.org/tapwater is a water test database that includes the results for many zip codes. If you're not on the list, get your water tested. Tap water often contains chlorine, fluoride, arsenic, lead, cadmium, mercury, and aluminum, all of which are harmful to your health. Any harmful ingredients you ingest must be dealt with by the body or stored. You can buy a water filtration system for your drinking water or even a whole house system.

Avoid Plastics

Plastics leach into your drinking water and food, and wreak havoc on your health. If you're going to use plastic, make sure it's BPA free, and don't leave it in the direct sunlight with your water in it. In an effort to stop using BPA, plastic manufacturers often use other chemicals that behave in the same way in the body. Make it a habit to bring your water with you wherever you go for the day in a glass or stainless steel container.

EMFs

Electromagnetic fields (EMFs) can create a harmful level of radiation in your home and work space. EMFs are created from technology devices and appliances that are plugged in to your electrical supply like: microwaves, washing machine, refrigerators, computers, cell phones, and lights. Devices created to offset these fields have been available for decades, but at the very least, don't sleep with electronics in your bedroom, and don't store your phone against your skin, in your bra, or even in your pocket. If you have a digital clock next to your bed with a light on it, replace it with an old-fashioned wind up or battery operated one that only lights up when you touch it.

Clothing

Wear natural fabric clothing on your skin—cotton, wool, silk, linen, bamboo, cashmere, and hemp are all great options. Avoid or limit the use of synthetic materials, such as polyester, nylons, and acrylics.

Unexpected Environmental Toxins

Clutter

Get rid of the clutter in your home and work space. It can take up more time and space physically, mentally, and emotionally than you realize. It takes more time to find things when they're not organized, by having to look through piles or move other things around to locate what you want. It can make you feel like you have too much to do or you're not getting enough done. All of this leads to more stress, and we know that stress triggers coping mechanisms, like eating, hiding, watching too much television, and so on.

Relationships

I'm including relationships here because they are so significant to reducing toxins in your life. What I've come to see is that some people get the diet right and clean up many of the toxins in their life, then if they still don't have the health they want, it's often because of one or more of their relationships. Although I'm not a relationship expert, this information comes from observation and experience.

> "Your task is not to seek for love,
> but merely to seek and find all the barriers
> within yourself that you have built against it."
> —*Rumi*

Just like everything else, first you stop the toxins. Begin by addressing any unresolved relationship issues or let them go. If you have a friend or relative that is particularly challenging, begin there.

Holding on to past pain and grievances (emotional toxins) can wreak havoc on your body. It can weaken your immune system, and cause anxiety and sleep loss. Clean up the past by detoxing your energy blockages, and making amends, or letting it go. If you're having a hard time letting something go, get some help. If you haven't been able to let go of a past grievance, enlist someone who can help, like a therapist or coach. It's amazing what the right words at the right time can do to change how you feel about a situation. Leaving things undone causes chronic stress in the body and wreaks havoc on your health.

In fact, Dan Buettner, author of *The Blue Zones*, interviewed centenarians around the world for *National Geographic*. He found the common denominators for longevity were: a plant-based diet, a sense of purpose in life, regular physical activity, and connection with friends and family. He said, "They all hang out with the right crowd; people who are healthy, happy, and trustworthy."

In relationships, one way to stop the toxins is to create space within yourself where you would otherwise have an immediate reaction. This is not to recommend that you run away from the situation, but by noticing the immediate emotional reaction within your body, you create the space to *choose* how you will respond, rather than going with an unconscious habitual reaction.

Breathe into the feeling and notice where you feel it. If you're very upset and in the fight-or-flight response, it's a perfect opportunity (because you have an alarm going off) to bring your awareness inside, before you say or do something that leads to further toxic emotions. Often, your biggest challenge in your life situation is your greatest gift. It can help you to live more fully, love more deeply, or see things in a new light.

Eckhart Tolle teaches that, "The way in which you perceive the other is determined by your own thought forms." This is so simple, but very powerful when you notice how you're feeling about your family member, partner, or friend. If you think that your partner is wonderful and focus on the good in them, you'll see them in a more forgiving and less judgmental light. If you focus on all the things they do that you don't like, you'll see them from a negative perspective. You get to choose.

Eckhart also teaches that the first step in relationship and life is to become present and allow. To become present means to stop thinking and focus all your attention on this moment, right now. For me, relationship has been my biggest teacher, as it's the place I would normally sacrifice myself for the good of others, ultimately serving no one. Thanks to the practice of staying present and deliberately going within when an emotional reaction takes over my body, I can more often process and handle the situation in a more loving way, which is a win/win for all involved.

Relationships can be the mirror for your inner work. We see others in our relationships as being outside ourselves, but what's going on outside you may be direct reflection of what's going on inside. There's no better place to recognize that than in your relationships. When I realized relationships were the mirror for my inner work, I began to see my partner showing me the things I needed to observe in myself. When you bring your awareness inside like that, it helps you shift your perspective from what the other person is doing wrong to "how can I relate". When you care for yourself and others the way you want to be cared for, things begin to change.

Notice how I said "care for yourself" at the beginning of that sentence? I mean, it's so easy to care for others, right? The hard part is to care for ourselves while still being fully present and loving. Being fully present can help you to learn to let go of positions that can keep you stuck reliving the same scenarios again and again.

I have become the Queen of Self-care, and everyone around me benefits from that. Now that I'm in my 50's, I know that when I first care for myself, I have more to give. I show up as my authentic self and I give permission for others to do the same. I'm also human. I'm not perfect nor do I need to be. I make mistakes. I'm not done. There's always room for improvement and expansion, but I believe it's what I do every day that counts most. I love being a rock for others and that begins with being stable. I am the most stable when I care for myself from the perspective of being responsible for my state of consciousness, so that I can connect more deeply, with more vulnerability, and without the need to defend or protect my position.

When you detox your inner and outer world, your life changes in a very significant way. You begin to see the magic in all things. There is a stillness there, a natural appreciation for life, with all its miracles and challenges.

CHAPTER 8

Celebrate Life

"The Soul unfolds itself,
like a lotus of countless petals."
—Kahlil Gibran

Vibrant health sets the stage for your life. Like a professional athlete or a chess player, it's what you bring to your next move that makes all the difference as to the experience you will have. When you take action from a healthy, grounded, confident position, you have upped the ante for your game.

You start with a desire to improve in some way: to feel better, have more energy, or heal something. Then you align with a solution, which in this case is detoxing. Then you educate yourself or find a mentor that resonates with you, whether it's a book or a program or a coach that can show you how. Then you must take action in order to change your health. When you feel better, your whole life is better, for yourself and for those around you and everyone around them, and so on and so on, like an interconnected web. You are only reading this book because you are expanding.

There is a part of you that will always continue to expand and create. As long as you're alive, you will never put your feet up, having arrived like a period at the end of the sentence. You may reach goals, live into and enjoy what you desire, but there will always be more. That's living. Living is expansive, until you leave your body and return to the field of pure potential. We are always expanding as part of an ever-expanding universe.

I was 17 when my brother died of cancer. He was 24. As his little sister, the thing I remembered most about him growing up was that he deeply loved and wanted to please our parents. He had a robust exuberance for life, which often led him to step outside his comfort zone. I remember him calling our Dad for advice on how to hang sheetrock for a job he'd gotten— before he knew how to do it. He worked at a busy bar at our local ski area doing standup comedy and impersonations, and then he'd play acoustic guitar and sing songs like the Beatles' "Rocky Raccoon." He never had a single lesson in music, but he possessed more courage than anyone I've ever met. He was so young, and he lived so full-out that it seemed absurd that he would become so ill.

If you have lost someone close to you to cancer, you know what I'm talking about. Watching them suffer and slowly disappear without being able to help is unbearable. After rounds of chemotherapy and radiation, having to pull to the side of the road for him to get sick after going out to lunch, watching his mustache and thick black hair disappear, and his broad capable body dwindle to nothing, was more than any of us knew how to cope with. And so... we didn't.

Until the morning came when we heard these short, definitive words from his doctor, "Jerry expired this morning." I remember feeling so blindsided at the lack of compassion in that word, "expired." To describe my brother, who had been so full of life, as though he were nothing more than an old carton of milk, literally took my breath away. My eyesight diminished to a narrow tunnel and I heard a deafening hum in my ears, like a train raging through my head. My knees went weak and I lost my ability to stand.

I have since come to understand that the oncologist was speaking to the fact that my brother was now lifeless, because when he was alive he was *inspired*. When he was alive, he was really alive. He had a big presence that he shared in his most authentic way. He truly lived. He took bold steps and sometimes he made mistakes, he laughed, he cried, he wanted to please, he hated, he loved, he gave it his all, and he put himself out there. He wasn't afraid to live.

Losing my brother to cancer is what inspired me to get on a path of natural wellness. I needed to see that there was another way to prevent and cure illness.

That inspiration has impacted thousands of people, you included. While suffering can be a door to awakening, being inspired is a more wonderful and joyful way to live. It feels good to be inspired. When we lift the layers that are keeping us from truly feeling what lies inside and feel the breath within us, inspiration rises out of that, enabling us to create or take action to improve a situation.

Whatever you create, whether it has a direct impact on others or not, is meaningless without connection. Imagine that you are on a planet all by yourself. Your primary concern, besides survival, would be to connect with someone or get yourself somewhere so it would be possible to connect with someone. Even a bird would have a dramatic impact on your existence if you were totally alone (even if you're someone who likes to be alone). Imagine that you're about to do that thing that you love to do. You paint a picture, build a house, or write a book. You jump up and down with the excitement for your accomplishment, but then the next thing you think of is that you want to share it with someone. You want someone who'll see it, use it, or enjoy it— whether it's while you're alive or even after you've gone.

I would venture to say that your personal health would not be that important to you without connection to other people, or the hope of it in the future. Would it matter if you had an extra 20 pounds to lose if you were going to spend the rest of your life completely alone?

Probably not. The one thing that brings meaning to our lives is connection. Having supportive, likeminded people that you feel safe with and can share your heart with is key when you want to be your healthiest self. It's like in the movie *Avatar*, when they say, "I see you." There is a sense of connection that somehow drops the need for hiding or covering up. You can be a whole being with all your baggage, and still be loved as you are. Recognize that and offer it to those around you.

You probably wouldn't have decided to detox to become more compassionate (neither did I); not because you're not a compassionate person, but changing our habits is often self-serving. The beautiful thing is that serving the self in this way does serve the other, as well. You are part of everything you experience. You have an impact on the world; without you it would be different. Realize that you are doing a lot by choosing to eat healthy food every day, because what you consume every day not only impacts how you look and feel, but it impacts others and the environment.

After you've been living from a mind, body, spirit detox perspective for a while, how you see the world changes. You may become more empathetic and find yourself not being able to kill a bug, or yell at someone. You may become more physically sensitive or feel more alive. Most people say they feel "clean" after detoxing. That's one reason I call this book *Lifting the Layers*.

After you've lifted a few layers, while caring for and fully occupying the energy field of the body, you feel more in tune with spirit, the spirit that rests in all beings.

Don't forget to acknowledge your wins. We are so accustomed to always looking at what we need to improve that we forget to celebrate what we did right. When you recognize your accomplishment with appreciation, you reward your own good behavior, and build positive momentum in the direction you desire to go.

Appreciate and feel gratitude for what you get to experience each and every day. Can you feel the difference these two words elicit in your body? Being grateful somehow puts you in a vulnerable receiving space by realizing that you have someone or something that adds to your life and makes it better. There's a drawing in or receiving quality to it. On the other hand, to appreciate something has an upward and outward feeling to it. When you appreciate something, you're holding it in high regard. You recognize and enjoy the good qualities of someone or something. There's a giving quality to it. It's a subtle internal shift in perspective to feel the difference between these two words. Both enhance how you feel and are available to you at all times.

Thank you. Without you, my work would be meaningless. Thank you for taking care of yourself, and in doing so, changing the world.

After Detox

"When I let go of what I am,
I become what I might be."
—Lao Tzu

Okay, so you've finished your 7-day (or more) commitment, you've lost a few pounds and probably a couple inches off your waist, and you need to know how to proceed. You don't want to detox for the rest of your life, but you don't want to go back to what you were doing and end up back where you started. Stop and take note of where you are:

How do you feel?

Have you shed a few pounds?

Have you recognized old thoughts that no longer server you?

Do you have more detoxing to do?

You're currently living the results of focused self-care. You've raised your awareness around what you consume, and you've been present more within your body over these last seven days, and as a result, you probably feel a lot better. It's amazing what seven days can do. Imagine what 30 days will do. You don't have to stop here.

The choices you make today will decide your tomorrow, because your future is determined by what you do right now. You don't have to be perfect, but let these last seven days make way for something to change, so that you're not just playing catchup next time.

Like waves shaping a rock, real change happens with continuous effort over time. To constantly see results with anything, you have to keep applying intention and attention. When you get into great physical shape, you can't stop exercising because you've arrived. Detoxing the mind (like exercising) isn't something you do once and forget about. When you take the time to do it regularly, you see results quickly. When it comes to the mind, there's always another layer to detox. So always be working on detoxing thoughts that no longer serve you as you recognize them. Pay attention to what you're thinking. When you become conscious of your thoughts, there's a degree of separation from them. It takes time to detox your mind, but it makes all the difference. It's like having all the right ingredients ready to make the perfect meal. If you start with fresh top-shelf ingredients, you're more likely to have a great result, but if you have a poison like arsenic in there or even the wrong spice, it can sabotage the whole recipe.

What can you take forward with you from these seven days? This is the beginning, not the end. You have just catapulted your health more than you can even possibly know at this moment, and you have before you a great opportunity. Remember, the wise shape their lives.

Ideas to Keep Moving Forward

- Keep reading your intention each morning for what you desire. Your intention will change as you reach your hopes and dreams. You'll have new ones, ever progressing in a deliberate direction and continuously improving your health and life. Remember, where your attention goes, energy flows. Ask yourself each night when you climb into bed, "What did I do today that I feel good about? What did I do today that brought me toward my intention?" Look for the things you did that are in alignment with your intention. Don't look for what you did that wasn't in alignment.

- Check in with yourself throughout the day and bring presence into your body. Set the timer on your phone to chime a few times during the day. When you hear the chime, remember to relax your body for a moment, focus on your breath and ask yourself, "Is what I'm currently doing going to take me *toward* where I want to go or *away* from it?"

- As much as possible, adhere to an organic plant based diet. You can reintroduce other whole foods back in, but do it slowly over time. If you go back to eating animal products, eat only organic and grass fed.

- Decide what habit(s) you want to adopt from these seven days, and keep it up. Whether it's having a whole foods fruits and vegetable shake or a vegetable juice every morning, a salad for lunch, or changing your snacks to fruits and vegetables, every one of these upgrades can make a big difference if you continue. Eat more plants, move more, stress less, and make more love.

- You don't have to be perfect to be conscious. Nobody is "perfect." There is no such thing and who would want to be? Life is meant to be lived. Don't get caught in the trap of thinking that you have to be perfect; it will keep you from feeling good about yourself and appreciating what you're doing right. When you try to be perfect and fail, then you get caught in the "I'll start tomorrow" story in your head, and that's a slippery slope, as you know. Allow yourself to have occasional foods that aren't necessarily detoxifying, and fully enjoy them. You can consciously choose to have a glass of wine, or a bowl of popcorn, or whatever it is that you enjoy. The more consciousness you bring in and the more deliberate you are with it, the better the "treat."

- Give thanks each evening for everything you can think of that day that you enjoyed, created, and shared. What you appreciate appreciates. Take the time to notice a giving and receiving experience with your food, your work, yourself, and other people in your life.
- Stay inspired. You can go back to old habits and end up back where you started, or you can take your new habits into your future. Consistency is key.

As I've written many times throughout this book, the results of what you are doing today will show up in your tomorrow. Think of detoxing like cleaning the windshield in your car. Sometimes you don't even realize how bad it is, or what a difference it will make, until you clean it. As the days progress, it gets even better. I recommend you do a detox at least four times per year. If you mark it on your calendar with the change of each season, it's easy to remember, and you'll be more in alignment with this beautiful Earth. Then keep at least one of your detoxifying practices with you after each detox, until it becomes a new habit or way of life.

Let this be the beginning of continuously learning and expanding. Read books, go to seminars, watch documentaries, and stay informed in a positive way. Don't get caught up in the negative side. Trust yourself. Don't pay attention to things that justify going back to old habits, because where your attention goes, energy flows. You can always find what you're looking for. Look for the light.

With Love,
Victoria Sol

References

Benson, Herbert, *The Relaxation Response.*
New York: HarperCollins, 2000.

Buettner, Dan, *The Blue Zones.* Washington, DC:
National Geographic Society, 2008.

CalleRodrigue, Rocio, Bala, Luis A., Hayes, Daniel
H., Farr, Gist H. Jr., *Southern Medical Journal*, "Primary Hepatic Lymphoma: A Case Report." Vol. 85, Issue 9, 1992.

Hanson, Rick and Mendius, Richard, *Buddha's
Brain.* Oakland, CA: New Harbinger Publications,
2009.

Hawkins, Sir David, *Power vs. Force.* Carlsbad, CA:
Hay House, 2005.

Katie, Byron, *Loving What Is.* New York: Random
House, 2002.

Lipton, Bruce. *The Biology of Belief: Unleashing
the Power of Consciousness, Matter and Miracles.*
Carlsbad, CA: Hay House, 2005.

Luskin, Fred, Stanford University study, 2005.
Siegel, Bernie, http:/ berniesiegelmd.com.

Sinek, Simon, *Start with Why.* New York: Penguin,
2009.

Heart Math "Quick Coherence Technique," https:/www.heartmath.com/quickcoherencetechnique.

Sabbatini, Riccardo, TED Talk: "How to Read the Human Genome and Build a Human Being," April, 2016. https:/www.ted.com/speakers/riccardo_sabatini.

International Agency for Research on Cancer, Group #1 Carcinogens. https:/en.wikipedia.org/wiki/List_of_IARC_Group_1_carcinogens.

Recommended Reading

Living Foods for Optimum Health: Staying Healthy in an Unhealthy World, by Brian R. Clement with Theresa Foy DiGeronimo

Diet for a New America 25th Anniversary Edition: How Your Food Choices Affect Your Health, Your Happiness, and the Future of Life on Earth, by John Robbins

The Power of Now, by Eckhart Tolle

The Tapping Solution: A Revoltioary System for Stress-free Living, by Nick Ortner (DVD also available)

The Plant-based Solution: America's Healthy Heart Doc's Plan to Power Your Health, by Joel Kahn

Made in the USA
Middletown, DE
21 November 2022

15640518R00088